A birth
into eternity

A birth into eternity

Tim and Coral Goddard

John Hunt
Publishing Limited

We will always be indebted to our families, friends, medics and countless other both here in the UK, in the US and further abroad, for their love, prayers, help and support during our 'Joshua Years'. We would not have survived without you all.

Also, a big thank you to those who encouraged and helped with the production of this book and with numerous proof readings, particularly to Dave Simmons and Bernard Cope.

Copyright © 2002 John Hunt Publishing Ltd

Text © 2002 Tim and Coral Goddard

ISBN 1 903019 79 6

Design: Andrew Milne Design

Write to: John Hunt Publishing Ltd, 46A West Street, Alresford, Hampshire SO24 9AU, UK

The rights of Tim and Coral Goddard, authors of this work, have been asserted in accordance with the Copyright, Designs and Patents Act 1988.

A CIP catalogue record for this book is available from the British Library.

Printed in Guernsey, Channel Islands

Visit us on the Web at: johnhunt-publishing.com

Contents

Preface

Thank you for picking up this book - if only to browse. We are an ordinary couple from London and these are our adventures with our first-born son. Assuming that you're going to read on, there are two things we would like to tell you in advance.

Firstly, there are sad bits. So you may find our story moving, and our frank style hard to read at times. But we chose such a style deliberately to convey the full reality of our experiences - good and bad - and to provide an alternative to biographies that skim over the less palatable aspects of life. Difficult things do happen and most people are unsure how they would respond if they - or someone they were close to - had a sick or terminally ill child. Yet many still want to know 'what it is like' and to be better informed. We likened our experience to a roller coaster ride, with plenty of high and lows, intensity and relaxation, happy and painful moments. By co-authoring the story we have presented the different perspectives of both mum and dad. Paradoxically, the hardest time in our lives has also been one of the most enriching, and given the choice, we would not have chosen any other way. It is our hope that this honest account of it all will give useful insight to those who want to know more about living through tragedy, and in some small way, give genuine reassurance and hope to any reader facing something similar.

Secondly, there are 'religious bits'. We are dedicated Christians and all we would ask of you is an open mind. Numerous people have asked us if what we went through caused us to doubt God. On the contrary, we found that our relationship with him took on new dimensions that it was the greatest possible source of strength and encouragement for us. So you'll find that we quote extracts from the Bible and songs that particularly influenced or helped us at crucial times. We found that what God had to say was practical and tangible, indeed integral, to our lives, rather than ethereal. Whether you have a faith or not, we hope you will be able to follow our spiritual journey in questioning and understanding the place of suffering.

Many around the world have described the positive impact our story has had on them already and it was the scale of this interest that spurred us to write. You may be surprised by the happy ending, not only throughout the restoration of hope for our future family following the birth of two healthy children, but also through dramatic spiritual experiences which transformed each of us emotionally, enabling us to be reconciled with our recent past. By the end, we suspect you may feel you know us very well. We offer you the totality of our experience, and hope that it intrigues and inspires you.

So let the roller coaster ride begin ...

Chapter One:

Great expectations

Tim Recounts

'I really did not expect it to happen like this!' It was ten thirty at night and I had been sent home to collect the bag that had been packed in anticipation just days before. Like most 'first time' expectant fathers, I had wondered when we would know that the 'right moment' had come to go to the maternity ward. I was shocked - I had only taken my wife Coral in for a check-up against dehydration. For weeks previously I had anticipated that moment over and over again in my mind. That prod in the ribs in the middle of the night to the words 'I think I'm in labour - should we go in?' We were three weeks away from D-day and Coral had had an upset stomach all day. I had come home from work early to look after her and when she didn't improve over the evening, we went to the hospital.

Having been banished under protest from the investigation room, I re-entered to find a flushed Coral greet me with the news that she was in labour! A strange disquiet came over us both. There was some measure of excitement, but we hadn't expected our first child to arrive so soon. The finishing touches to the nursery had only been completed the day before! Christmas was hardly over and Coral had been looking forward to a few more weeks at home, as it felt like her maternity leave had only just begun. So, I was dispatched home to collect the bag containing the baby's things, while Coral settled into her room in the isolation unit due to concern about a possible infection being the cause of the stomach problems.

Nearly eight months earlier, a few days after discovering that Coral was pregnant, we had been lying on a beach in Portugal discussing baby names and had immediately hit on 'Joshua' if we had a boy.   Our friends John and Wendy Pattison were also expecting their first imminently at that time and had inspired us by the fact that they had prayed over which name to give their child. My initial reaction had been 'humph - how super spiritual', but as the notion settled, we thought how right it was to ask God's help in choosing a name appropriate for our 'yet to be born' child.   Even after just two years of marriage, friends laughed at our ability to want opposite things and they were often entertained by the ensuing banter. For Coral and I both to agree to something straight away was a rare occurrence and made us think that it must be God at work in us when it happened that way! Characteristically, we could not settle on a girl's name throughout the rest of the pregnancy, but 'Joshua' was never dethroned from our number one choice for a boy. My wife had a feeling that she was carrying a boy and really wanted a boy, coming from a family of three girls as she did. I too secretly wanted a boy, but maintained an 'I don't mind what we have, it's more important that it's healthy' stance to the world.

Lying out on the beach in Portugal, we were still in a state of shock over the pregnancy. A little more than a month previously we had been told by Coral's gynaecologist that we were likely to have trouble conceiving. If we wanted to start a family straight away, fertility drugs were recommended. We had gulped, declined the drugs in preference to 'trusting God' initially, only to find that Coral fell pregnant the next month! Little did we realise to what depths we would learn to trust God over the ensuing years. Life was going swimmingly for us - the archetypal 'yuppies', both with lucrative City jobs with leading but rival UK High Street banks. We had a spacious two-bedroom flat, a good church and great friends. Falling pregnant so soon was not quite as planned, as we were still in the process of buying our dream house and we anticipated that we would need Coral's salary for longer to overcome the expenses of moving. Still, after a short while we were very happy, with all the wonder of pregnancy, of this little life form developing inside. And for me, I was content, as the early pregnancy symptoms of tiredness and nausea meant that the usually manicly active Coral had relented on wanting to see the whole of Portugal in ten days and was quite happy to rest on the beach instead.

Trying to buy this house was proving to be particularly complex and hassled and I was worn. I was very conscious however that God was teaching us some powerful lessons through it all about His sovereignty, the significance of which we had no idea of at the time. With hindsight, I can see how much God built in me of direct relevance and help for what was to come. At the time though, I felt as if I was being put through the mill.

Back at the hospital we settled down for the night. We both felt a nervous excitement as I squeezed Coral's hand. We flicked through a few more girls' names, but didn't settle on anything. I picked up the book on childbirth, which I had thought I'd have time to read properly whilst commuting into London. Oh well, what I didn't know now, I soon would see and the images from the hospital's 'Parentcraft' evenings flashed through my mind. Midwives pushing dollies out of football socks, breathing routines, the emphasis on how long and slow labour was in most cases.

It was 7.00 a.m. Tuesday 5th January, 1993. Coral had wanted an 'active' labour - the ability to keep walking around, have
baths and knowing her, the chance to practise her latest aerobics
routine! But after a night of being hooked up to monitors and
drips, this was clearly not going to be an option. She was already
feeling drained and tired and the show had hardly begun. So
reluctantly we agreed to hospital intervention and we transferred
to the delivery room for the start. Two midwives were assigned
to us, one experienced, one a student - her first ever delivery.
They scurried around taking the dust covers off everything, for
we were in a Labour room attached to the isolation unit, which
had hardly ever been used. It was a strange feeling, looking
around the sterile room, the equipment, monitors, dressing
packs, the bed, thinking 'this is where our first child is going to
enter the world'. I phoned our families with the news of the
impending arrival as they awoke to start their days and met with
the usual excitement. Perhaps it was the sleepless night, but the
whole thing seemed surreal. Time was almost standing still.

And so it did. At various points I left the room to feed money
in the meter in the car park, or back to Coral's room to pick out
the first outfit our baby was to wear. Coral had been given
Pethidine and was mostly unaware of who or what was in the
room by this point, until a contraction came. Then she knew
about pain! The experienced midwife told us that she wanted the
student to deliver the baby, if that was OK with us. The pregnancy had been remarkably good, with no indication that anything was wrong and we had no objection so long as the
experienced nurse stayed around. All the ante-natal checks had
shown that a very strong and lively baby was on its way and we

were expecting nothing less. Those poor girls. The labour progressed quite rapidly now thanks to the introduction of the hormone though Coral's drip. However, the drugs seemed to make Coral even more drowsy and the pain all the more intense. I felt so subdued, why couldn't I feel excitement like I should? I decided I really did want that boy - secretly hoping for a 'son and heir', a phrase my late father had used so frequently during my childhood that it seemed to be part of my bones.

It approached 11.00 a.m. and Coral entered the second stage. She was allowed to push at last but just as the labour had progressed so too had her levels of exhaustion. Finally, as our baby's head began to crown, the two midwives and I exchanged anxious glances. Something was clearly wrong, as there seemed to be large brown circles on its head. But before we could catch proper looks, Coral's exhaustion caused the push to end and the head to recede. As the student midwife felt for the cord around the baby's neck she became worried and the experienced nurse took over. Immediately, she told Coral to stop pushing - an excruciating command for any woman to hear at that stage of labour. A button was pressed and the room filled with some other doctors and nurses. I began to feel a knot in my stomach, as my subdued anticipation gave way to full-blown anxiety. Still Coral was instructed not to push as they checked the neck once more. Worried glances were exchanged between the medics and myself, but no one said anything. Clearly they were confused, as it felt like the cord was around the baby's neck, but not quite.

The only words exchanged were between Coral, desperate to push and get this baby out - herself totally unaware of anything being wrong and the midwife, encouraging her to hold off. Everyone apart from Coral could now clearly see the baby's head, blond hair faintly covering numerous large and varied brown circles on the scalp. The medics then decided to get the baby out quickly, but Coral's exhaustion was immense. Forceps were mentioned and the threat of them gave sufficient impetus to Coral to deliver the baby with the next contraction.

'It's a boy' I remember calling to Coral, as every faculty in my body tried to assimilate the shock of what I was seeing. The horror was tangible around the room. In that moment my joy of having a son was the only positive emotion.

'It's a boy Coral. You've given me the son I've always wanted.' I choked.

My mind and emotions froze at the shock of what I was seeing. Our little Joshua started crying immediately, scored the top marks on all the Apgar Score and he weighed a healthy 6lb 15oz, despite being three weeks early. Yet this baby was like nothing I or the assembled paediatricians and midwives had ever seen before.

'Have you decided on a name yet?' the midwife called to us through the haze of shock.

'Yes, Joshua,' I replied with a pride that months of anticipation of naming a son had built up, yet made hollow by the stronger and more real emotions of grief and shock. This moment was not something we had expected or bargained for. The doctors and midwives scurried around him while Coral remained exhausted and semi-conscious on the bed.

The brown circular marks on the baby's scalp gave way to continuous red, raw and bleeding tissue from the back of the head, the neck, the whole of his little back and down to the back of his knees. Particularly around the neck and upper back, there were numerous lumps of varying sizes and colours, from a few millimetres through to three to four centimetres. They formed a little hunchback of tissue just above a gaping hole. He looked as if he had lain in acid, as the flesh on his back and neck was so raw and contused. As he was turned over I saw that his face too was covered with these brown marks, including a teardrop of brown lumpy flesh over the left corner of his mouth. His tummy had more white skin, but his little arms and legs were covered with yet more fleshy mounds of brown tissue akin to sweatbands of flesh around his wrists and ankles. The doctor had bundled him into a cloth, held him up for Coral to see then rushed him and me down to the Special Care Baby Unit on the floor below. Coral, still hazy with drugs and without her contact lenses, saw vaguely her new-born son, identified that he had brown marks on his back and then drifted off into an uneasy but desperately needed oblivion of sleep.

Joshua opened his eyes and gazed at me for the first time. I will never forget the preciousness of that moment. He was less than half an hour old and lying quite contentedly in his 'fish tank' - our nickname for the clear Perspex cots they use for the newborn. These two deep blue pools seemed to communicate in volumes. He seemed to drink in every detail of my face and I felt an immense love and feeling of pride well up in me for him. In those few moments we had bonded. He did not have much of a forehead or chin at that stage, due to the pressures of birth and so he had an endearing similarity to ET! Apart from his skin he was doing well, but no one in our local hospital had seen such a baby before, neither could they tell us what was wrong. The state of shock was still intense. I was numb, crying, feeling a physical pain, yet strong love for my child and wife all at the same time. My thoughts turned to Coral upstairs, still in the Labour ward.

What was she feeling; what did she know? How would she react?

'Oh Lord, help her!' I sighed. Here was Coral, the career and fitness woman, who had loved being pregnant, but was very dubious about being around babies and children until they were old enough to communicate with. On top of that, appearance and good looks had been strongly held values in her own family upbringing and our new-born, whilst beautiful, was covered in such disfiguring marks. My instincts told me to break the news to her piecemeal. Apart from anything, the medics were at a loss as to what to diagnose. I returned to the Labour ward to assure Coral that Joshua was holding his own well downstairs. He had various monitors all over him, but they were recording a strong heart and lungs. I told her that he had brown marks over him, but that he had these large beautiful blue eyes, just like his mum. By this stage, Coral was exhausted, sore and drugged and need-ed some sleep. From her lack of reaction, I was not sure whether she even understood what I was saying.

We transferred back to her private room across the corridor, this time grateful that the suspected stomach infection had afforded us such accommodation separate from other healthy births and Coral settled down to get a few hours' sleep. I returned to Joshua, desperate to do something, but unable to change a thing. Already the immense love I felt created a desire to protect and fight for him.

In a few short hours, our lives and expectations had been turned upside down and I was in free fall. Still gasping for breath and attempting to assimilate the magnitude of what had just hap-pened, thoughts, emotions, questions rushed through my mind at breakneck speed without lodging. Through the shock, I told the nurse that I needed to make a few phone calls and headed for the payphone in the corridor.

'There's no need to use that phone. Here, make your calls from my office' she offered 'and I'll bring you a cup of tea.' As the nurse returned and passed me the mug, I noticed that it had a verse from the Bible on it:

My Grace is sufficient for you.[1]

This was more than just a coincidence. If ever there was a time I was desperate for God's help, it was now. 'God, help me,' I breathed.

---

[1] *2 Corinthians 12 v 9*

Chapter Two:

A Mum for how long?

Coral Recounts

When I eventually awoke, Tim pushed me down the corridors in a wheelchair at about 5 o'clock that evening. I had not seen Joshua clearly when he was born but I knew something was terribly wrong. Our baby was being held in the Special Care Baby Unit (SCBU) and I was very afraid of what we would find when we got there. All the way, Tim was trying to prepare me for the worst and in my imagination I was expecting to meet with such deformity that I was not thinking much about the little person himself who was waiting there for me. My stomach was churning with fear and dread and I could not stop wondering; 'Would he even be still alive?' As we went into yet another lift, the trek through the hospital seemed interminable.

Finally, Tim wheeled me through the door and we were ushered through the main ward with all the premature babies, flashing lights and beeping, into a side room with three little plastic tanks. Only one of them was occupied and it was immediately obvious, here was our baby.

Inevitably, I wept when I saw his poor little body. But even before I saw his face I was overwhelmed with a sense of love for him. First I saw the hole in the middle of his back, the lumps all over it and the black, red and purple mounds around the back of his neck like different shiny berries, the spots of his blood on the sheets. It was as terrible as Tim had described but all I could

think was 'he's mine' and through my tears, I managed to ver-
balise, 'He's going to need so much love and I'm the one that's
going to give it to him.'

Even then, it seemed wrong to pity him. Something about
him immediately suggested that he had strength and his eyes
when they opened were unbelievable. They were gigantic, darkest indigo, uncannily knowing and somehow taking everything in
already. My first impulse was to pick him up and feed him myself
but I was surprised when the nurses agreed. He was carefully
wrapped in his bloodied sheet and passed to me. Then I felt
proud that with very little help, I managed to latch him on. I had
to. There were too many other problems to have trouble with
breastfeeding, so I hardly noticed how much it hurt or the fact
that he was not properly latched on at all! He was certainly getting the milk and fed with a strong suck. I also noticed how he
kicked with such force. It was the same movements I had been
feeling inside my stomach and the same vigorous kick that struck
out at the midwives when they had tried to listen for the baby's
heartbeat in the ante-natal clinic. Although visually so different
from what I expected or wanted, the little character that I had
got to know when inside of me was now the same little bundle
feeding ferociously at my breast. It was as though we already
knew each other.

As well as proud, I was also shocked, devastated and confused.
Surely he could not live looking the way he did and yet he was so
strong, how could he die? I found myself praying quietly in my
head, 'Either heal him or take him Lord. Just don't let me develop a relationship with this little one if You are going to take him,
because it would be too painful and too much for me to bear.' I
reasoned that it would be easier if he died early, rather than later

in childhood. After all, a tiny baby has very little personality to begin with. But the bond was already there.

As I studied Joshua, I was searching every area of his body for a hand or foot or anything that might have escaped the reddish brown marks. But they were everywhere. Even a toe and an entire finger were engulfed by the abnormal skin. I longed for just one bit to be perfect but nothing had escaped this dreadful thing. I cried some more and then through the tears we laughed at how already he was lifting his head to try and look around. From the books I had read, I felt sure that was not meant to happen yet but what did I know about such things?

That night I was compelled to keep checking on him, unsure if he would even make it through the night. So I made my way through the corridors several times. This baby utterly depended on me and I was going to be there right from the start. Above everything else, if he lived, he would need a strong sense of security that would only come from feeling utterly loved and accepted. He would be the object of people's stares and rejection, so right then I determined I would give my child so much love that when others rejected him, he would be less affected by it. He was my son, he was special and I would love him with everything I had. In truth, Joshua drew out of me more selfless love than I ever knew I was capable of giving.

The next morning, I was filled with dread to realise I had not been dreaming. It felt more like a nightmare than reality, as I gradually came round, especially as this child was not even expected to be born for another three weeks. Such was my disbelief, I even felt my tummy to check that the baby was no longer there! I wished I was still pregnant with the hope of a healthy child inside and I even missed the uncomfortable kicking and squirming inside me. But no, that special time of carrying my child had ended all too abruptly and this was not the result anyone expected. I was struck by fear. How would I ever cope? In such a desperate situation, it was not surprising that my thoughts naturally turned to God. Then it came to me almost immediately. Somewhere in the Bible I had once read that the Lord does not give us more than we can cope with. I did not know the exact verse or even where to find it but I knew that it was there and it was God's specific encouragement to me right then.[2]

Wow! God actually thinks I can cope with this! He must have a high regard for me if he thinks I will manage this one!

'Well Lord, if you say I can do it then I'd better get on with it!' Suddenly, the fear evaporated and it was oddly replaced by excitement; to think I'd been singled out for such a difficult task and chosen to be Joshua's mum. It made me feel very special and gave me a very tangible inner strength, which was to carry me through the week to follow.

I knew the best thing I could do was to concentrate on positive thoughts and there were plenty of them, like thanking God we had a boy not a girl; surely disfiguration is somehow harder for a girl I reasoned. Then thanking God he had chosen to put Joshua into our home, though by no means perfect, at least we were a family that had sufficient faith, material wealth and maturity to be able to raise him in a loving and stable environment. Then, still in the quietness of my hospital room I found I was telling myself the truth of the Bible that, *'In all things God works for the good of those who love Him, who have been called according to His*

---

[2] *1 Corinthians 10 v 13: 'And God is faithful; he will not let you be tempted beyond what you can bear. But when you are tempted, he will also provide a way out so that you can stand up under it.'*

purpose.'[3]

I was still experiencing many mixed emotions. In SCBU the staff called me 'mum' and I found that hard to accept. Silently, I reacted against my new title. After all, why even aspire to such status if it was soon to be taken away from me? There were times that I felt the staff there did not appreciate the horror I was feeling. I kept thinking 'Elephant man' and 'Hunchback of Notre Dame'. My baby would be seen as a freak if he lived at all. But to them Joshua was the largest baby in the unit among all the premature children and his vital signs were all normal and healthy.

As Joshua had a large ulcer in the centre of his back, we were advised not to dress him. Then when he was three or four days old, I found him there lying on his sore back, all upset and with someone's clothes on. I was incensed. Who did this? How could they? Before he was born, I had dreamed of dressing my baby and had chosen the first outfit he was to wear. How dare they? Surely they knew about the ulcer in his back, the risk of infection and his bleeding neck. They should have asked me first. Tim came in to find me angrily undressing Joshua and once again in tears.

My shock had turned to anger as I had visions of him in permanently bloodied clothes. What were we going to do? One day at a time, I reminded myself. To look any further ahead was self-induced torture. That day, my sister was coming to visit and I was looking forward to seeing her. As my younger sister Donna is also a nurse, she was granted the concession of becoming one of Joshua's first visitors in the SCBU. When she saw him, her reaction took me totally by surprise.

---

[3] *Romans 8 v 28*

'He's beautiful Coral!' What a strange thing to say, I thought, but oh so reassuring. She had seen past the disfiguring lumps and marks and was actually seeing my baby for something else. 'He looks like Tim but he's got your eyes,' she continued, almost as though she needed to pursue her point. I was so glad it was possible for someone else to see beyond the ugliness and to respond with more appreciation than sympathy. Though we had seen it too, we had got used to seeing people's horror already and hardly dared hope anyone else might find him remotely cute. The disfiguring lumps were just too obvious and too extreme.

There were so many unanswered questions but the question of 'Why me?' seemed a futile and negative one that I deliberately chose not to dwell on. It would only set me onto a negative spiral and anyway, why NOT me? Everything else in my life had been rather perfect just lately so it was God's prerogative to change that for the good of all. After all, the world is not perfect and bad things happen all the time. Why should I be immune from hardship? I believed God would continue to give me the ability to cope and that if I focused on Him, I could grow and learn from the experience. Or, I could look at the situation and become bitter. The choice was obvious and I know now that it was God Himself who strengthened me at this time and helped me to see all this so clearly. I could not have got through that week in such a good state of mind if it had not been for His very real power in my life to help me see things the way I did.

I was grateful that nine years earlier I had responded to God by inviting Him to take control of my life. Apart from Sunday School as a child I had had little contact with Christians or church up to that point. The night I met with God was something of a dramatic and miraculous occasion. I happened to go to a big evangelistic celebration meeting with a friend of my boyfriend at that time. I was there for all the wrong reasons as I had mainly gone for the ride on a motorbike and to make my boyfriend jealous! I had no idea what to expect and little did I know that what would confront me there would be a throng of people dancing as they sang songs of worship! They really were worshipping, which I had never seen before. Something was different about their faces.

So caught up were they in singing to God that no one was really looking at me and I was free to do my own thing which was to listen and read very carefully the words of the songs. There was such a truth in the lyrics that I found it hard to argue. Yet argue I did. All evening I found myself wrestling with why this sort of thing would not work for me. Each time another excuse came into my head, the preacher had an uncanny way of answering the very thing I was thinking. So, finally, I ran out of excuses and the moment he said that God had been speaking to people there that night, I realised that was what it must have been. Just as he suggested, I surrendered my struggling with my life to the One who made everything, including me. I think the realisation that swayed me was that Jesus loved me so much that He died for me, even though He knew how terrible I had been.

Here was someone who would give me a new start and purpose if I would recognise my failure and turn to Him. Trying to live my life without including God so far had got me nowhere, that much was suddenly clear. So the preacher was right. It was all in the Bible and God would continue to give me directions in life if I gave Him the control, which was rightfully His anyway. I knew instantly things would be different and they still are.

My boyfriend noticed a change in me straight away and he

himself went along to church the next week and made a similar response. Quite quickly and without anyone's prompting we realised that we felt wrong about living together unmarried and, as we were only twenty at the time, we separated. He eventually moved back to America and some time later I met and married Tim. But that was by no means the only change.

Gone were the wild parties that had failed to change my unhappiness for very long, if at all. Gone too was a lot of the desperate insecurity, the feeling that I had to please everyone all of the time and instead came a whole new way of living which is still improving as I listen to God's teaching and the Holy Spirit. Left to my own devices I would probably be in clinical depression by now, or on hard drugs. It was as though my eyes were opened and I started to see everything from a different perspective. The world was a beautiful place after all and it was only people like me, doing our own selfish thing that was messing it up and causing life to be a struggle.

So I always continue to thank God that He gave me a new way of living that unsuspecting evening. Without His intervention and work of change in me I would not have been the person I am today and would definitely not have had the God-given resources to face the challenges that our first-born was to bring.

Chapter Three:
Even though He slay me...

Tim Recounts

Back at home the evening Joshua was born, the shock of the day was still intense. There was a strong temptation to deny it all, to pretend that the day hadn't happened, that Coral was still pregnant and would soon give birth to a healthy baby. As I set about making phone calls, everything within me wanted not to. Naturally enough, the people I was calling were at first elated as I said 'Coral has had her baby.' At three weeks premature, people weren't expecting such news just yet. Time and time again, I would have to burst their bubble of delight with the second part of the story. 'Yes, but Joshua has got something badly wrong with his skin.' Time and time again, the conversation became emotional as I worked hard to get them to understand it was serious and both parties reeled from the impact of the day's events. What made matters even worse was the lack of diagnosis from the medics, leaving me to give gruesome descriptions as best I could and answer the same questions every time. They had never seen such a condition before and were saying absolutely nothing about what might be wrong or what could have caused such a condition. I was unable to communicate anything to our friends and relatives other than how Joshua's skin looked.

With hindsight, making those phone calls was a very necessary part of my own coming to terms with the reality and accepting it, no matter how much I wished the reality was something else. The sense of pain was intense - it felt more like a bereavement than a birth and in one sense Coral and I both knew it was just that - we were grieving the healthy baby we had anticipated.

Needless to say, sleep eluded me that night. My mind was racing. The adrenaline pumped furiously. Early on I faced the 'Why' question and decided that it wouldn't lead me anywhere useful. But through the turmoil God began to speak. Sentences from the Bible began to race through my mind, some of them I'd learnt in childhood and not read since.

"The Lord gives, the Lord takes away, blessed be the name of the Lord" [4] *and "even though He slay me, yet will I trust Him."* [5]

The Bible story of Job was such an example. I was very conscious of having a choice of how to respond to the arrival of Joshua: to turn to God or to turn against God in anger and inevitable bitterness. Earlier on in life I had learnt that bitterness only damages yourself and in many cases the bitterness becomes more of a problem than the incident from which it stems. Still, right now could I honestly say, 'blessed be the name of the Lord'?

The months of pregnancy rushed through my mind - it had all been so normal, nothing had happened which could have damaged the baby. Coral had kept so well she had continued to teach aerobics in the evenings until 7 months - only a few weeks before Joshua's birth. As this was our first baby, maybe we were genetically incompatible? Too many unanswerable questions! The only

[4] *Job 1 v 21*   [5] *Job 13 v 15*

thing I could conclude with any certainty was that God wasn't to blame, as He didn't intend life to be imperfect in any way. The marring effect of something less than perfection and the suffering of the innocent is something to get angry about, but to turn against God would be targeting the wrong person and would only compound the injustice already done.

I was born into a Christian, God-fearing family and my parents encouraged each of their four children to read the Bible at home from an early age. I had been taught that sin, suffering and imperfection were the results of humanity's fallen nature. God had created us and our world perfect and had wanted it to stay that way. Man had chosen to leave the idyll, using his freedom of choice to do things 'his own way'. Yet God is ultimately in control and so had, for whatever reason, allowed Joshua's condition.

What a mystery the sovereignty of God is! I knew I couldn't and can't answer it and it's a frequent reminder to me that God is bigger than my tiny mind and intellect. So one thing became clear to me. It was my response that mattered and all that I had control of. Turning against God would only compound the problem, which was awful enough as it was. 'Biting the hand that feeds you' was the phrase that seemed to sum it up for me. So I determined to try and be like Job of the Bible, who in the face of adversity still turned to God in worship. In the middle of his trouble he could say: 'blessed be the name of the Lord.'

Along with Job, I recognised that God allows both good and bad even though He never intended His creation to become imperfect. I determined not to allow this awful tragedy to come between me and God.

I was also very mindful of another verse in Psalm 51, which

speaks of God requiring *'truth in my innermost being'*[6] . I had to face my own desire to try to block out the reality of Joshua's condition and accept it fully, even though it was unnamed and unquantified. I had to face my own sense of hurt and pain and be honest before God rather than pretend that all was OK, or to be supercilious. I cried so much in those early days and nights (and this was the guy who as a teenager had resolved crying was for wimps!). And yet it was not with a sense of despairing hopelessness. I found that being real before God about my shock and pain was the route to comfort and strength.

Other Bible verses came to mind: Psalm 23 assured me of God's presence even when we walk through the *'valley of the shadow of death.'*[7] Joshua's skin looked so broken and bleeding, that I could not help but question whether he would survive. Already the question mark over whether it was the 'big C' (cancer) had crossed my mind. Questions over life expectancy jarred me to the core. Everything about a birth speaks of life and longevity. To question whether a baby will live feels like driving into a brick wall at 100 mph. You just don't expect that thought. We certainly did not know whether our new-born was going to survive, but that night God was gracious enough to pour His comfort into my emotions. As I turned towards God, the assurance that He was with me and my family, was very tangible.

The promises that no situation is too hard for God are numerous in Scripture and many of them came flooding into my thoughts. As my overactive mind thought of new questions, new 'what ifs', so the assurance from other parts of the Bible brought strength and resolve, as the Holy Spirit brought them to memo-

---

[6] *Psalm 51 v 6*   [7] *Psalm 23 v 4*

ry. In the apostle Paul's letter to the Romans, he wrote that nothing *'can separate us from the love of God.'*[8] And certainly, I knew we would all need that intimacy with Him to get through the unknown future.

I jumped from issue to issue in illogical fashion. Irrationally I found myself also worrying about how other children would react to Joshua at school, because he looked so different and then Isaiah 53 flashed through my mind, *'He (Jesus) was despised and rejected by men.'*[9]

There was this dual edge to my emotions. A real sense of pain at how others might react to my son in years to come, yet a real strength from knowing that even in this, Jesus had experienced everything in much greater measure than we ever would. He could empathise and help us succeed too. Other verses such as *'Man looks at the outward appearance, but the Lord looks on the heart'*[10] reminded me sharply that our thinking and standards are out of line with God's. It made me realise from the start that Joshua, as a person, was far more important than how he appeared. Whilst we should do all we could for his appearance, focusing on his own sense of being loved, feeling secure, valuing his personality and honing his behaviour and values were the more important goals. It dawned on me that to give him love, security and acceptance was the best thing any parent could do for a child.

So it continued. As fresh worries and questions stung me, so fresh words from the Bible would bring soothing reassurance of God's ever-present help. It was like the swirling of oil and vinegar in a salad dressing. As the acidity of reality stung my emotions, the oil of God's presence assured me of God's ability to

[8] *Romans 8 v 39* [9] *Isaiah 53 v 3* [10] *1 Samuel 16 v 7*

face the 'unfaceable' with us.

As our families and friends heard our news, I knew that many of them would be praying. That is why I believe I was so conscious of God's help just then.

'What kind of dad could willingly sacrifice the life of his own son?' I thought, as I began to experience fatherhood for myself. Every instinct in me was to hold and protect my son. Yet God chose to give his Son up to death in order to buy us back. How torn God must have felt in His emotions.

The wonder at the new-born is so precious. Those tiny fingers and toes, the little face that changes shape during the first twenty-four hours (why didn't anyone tell us that?). As an expectant father, I had dutifully put my hand on Coral's tummy when she had felt him kicking and I had read the books with her, which described each stage of development, but nothing compared with actually seeing him and realising that here was this little person to care for, get to know and love. As I thought of his little body, fresh memories of other deformities came to mind. What were those black stye-like lumps on his neck? 'He must be in pain, yet he's so quiet,' I thought.

That first night I also worried about Coral again. Surely, after such a traumatic event she would become depressed postnatally. After all it was a common experience for many new mums with healthy babies. What if she rejected him or didn't bond? What an introduction to motherhood for the career girl. Being apart at night was hard, so all that could be done was to pray that God would provide her with all she needed right now. What a sense of relief the next day to find her so bright and to hear what the Lord had encouraged her with during the night. She developed such a deep love for Joshua that any fears on my part about rejection were clearly unfounded and in the weeks and months to come there was not a trace of depression to be found despite the ever increasing pain and anguish.

Fresh anxiety came during the second day from the doctor.

'In order to try to determine the nature of the skin tissue, we'd like to take a skin puncture biopsy from Joshua's back. It involves anaesthetising a local area and cutting a piece of tissue away so we'll need your consent.' In the actual event, it was difficult for us to see where the doctor had removed tissue, as so much of his back and neck was bleeding anyway. The initial shock lessened but our brains went further into overdrive with questions. What was wrong with his skin? What had happened in the womb? Did anyone keep the placenta or catch any of the amniotic fluid? Was it acidic? Why couldn't anyone tell us anything? Little did we realise that we were beginning a path of living with unanswered questions and pushing medics for solutions and resolve that would become a very normal way of life for us. We felt vulnerable about how people might react and were reassured as people responded with compassion.

My sister-in-law Donna was working nights as a nurse and had wanted to visit Coral the next day, but I had forgotten to return her call. So I called her at work in the early hours of the Thursday to set up her visit for that afternoon, as she had wanted. During the conversation she asked me something which caught me by surprise. Had this caused me to doubt my faith? After twenty-four hours of feeling the presence of God's strength and comfort so tangibly amidst our pain, the question felt like one of those jolts we were getting used to. I don't know to this day what she made of my reply!

'Why should it?' I heard myself say. 'My faith is based on the fact that Jesus died and rose again 2000 years ago so that we can have a relationship with God today, not on what happens to us. Rather than turning from God, Coral and I are turning to Him. He's the only one who can ultimately make the difference for Joshua and for us.' Looking back on that time, the enormity of God's interaction with us was so special and humbling and there was so much clear evidence of His love for each of us. It was a reminder that we can each receive from His inexhaustible supply of love; it's a matter of us turning to Him and tuning in.

The staff in the maternity unit allowed us to stay in their isolation wing, which was a real benefit, as it accorded us privacy away from the noise and bustle of the healthy new-borns and mums. Coral's large room quickly filled with cards, presents and flowers.

As the days passed we became more and more anxious to get news from the doctors and the lack of information was frustrating. On numerous occasions I got angry with them about the time it was taking to get the biopsy results or to find anything which might give clues. One of the Senior Registrars brought in a gigantic medical encyclopaedia with hundreds of pictures of various birth defects and together we pored over it late one night. I found a picture of an older baby's back, which looked something like Joshua's and the description, frustratingly short, said 'melanocytic naevus containing malignant melanoma'. Once more I had the sense of being thumped in the stomach. My fear over cancer loomed up.

'Has Joshua got cancer?' I asked.

'No, I doubt it very much indeed. You can't get skin cancer in the womb. It's just not heard of for babies to be born with cancer.' My intellect was reassured, but a scripture buzzed through my mind: *'and Mary kept these things and pondered them in her heart'.*[11]

'What are you saying, Lord?' I asked. Since Joshua's birth I had been asking God for wisdom over Joshua, his condition and treatment. My constant prayer had been, 'Please warn me God of what is to come, so that I can best prepare myself and then prepare how best to tell Coral.' My instincts were that Joshua's condition was cancerous and no matter how reassuring the doctor had been, I guessed I should do as Mary and 'keep these things in my heart' until proven otherwise at least.

A mind in shock doesn't think straight and trying to remember all the questions I'd thought of over the preceding days and hours in preparation for the doctors' round, was not possible without help. Having our church pastors and good friends John and Dawn Singleton there was invaluable in reminding us of the important things we'd said we needed to ask, as well as adding important aspects of their own.

As that first week of Joshua's life in SCBU was nearing its end and the local doctors were preparing to send us home. I had to insist on a referral to the Hospital for Sick Children, Great Ormond Street in London (GOS), one of the best paediatric specialist centres in the country, if not the world.

'You won't get an appointment straight away,' 'Joshua is a strong baby,' and 'You'll have to wait for an appointment' came the reply, to which I retorted with:

'But what condition does my son have? What should we do with the now ulcerated lesion on his back?'

In the face of their 'Don't knows', the assertive but stubborn

---

[11] *Luke 2 v 19*

side of my character emerged as I stuck with demanding an immediate referral to GOS.

Eventually we won through and an appointment was made for the following Monday with one of the two Consultant Dermatologists at GOS; Doctor John Harper. We were to be transferred by ambulance. With some sense of relief that we had made progress, we waited for the Monday and in the meantime, continued to fall in love with our son, worry over what we saw, but also chuckle with delight as we watched the hilarious faces he pulled before burping and his little but strong personality begin to emerge. Monday was also the day of the skin puncture biopsy results.

That Sunday was an important day for me. Not only were our families in a state of shock, but so too was our church family. Most people had already heard the news and in the months leading up to Joshua's birth, Coral and I had headed up the welcoming teams on Sunday mornings, so we were also well known to those who were 'just visiting' the church, as well as the regular members. It had the potential to be hard for me, as so many people were affected by our news and wanted to express their support. Yet I knew that I wanted to go to church and to worship God. It was a conscious decision, a statement, not to let this traumatic event come in the way of my relationship with God.

During the week I had sought to worship on my own, yet I knew that it would also be an important step to do so publicly at church. So, on my way to the Hospital I slipped into the church meeting when the worship was already in progress and knelt. I don't remember which songs were being sung, but I do remember my determination to tell the Lord how much I loved Him and how much I was grateful for His sensitivity and tenderness to

Coral and me during the shock of the preceding week. I resolved that day not to allow the tragedy of Joshua's skin condition to come between God and me. I reckoned that enough suffering had been perpetrated already without any potential bitterness towards God on my part adding to the problem. It was a pretty intimate time with the Lord, alone, yet surrounded by people worshipping God.

By being there that morning, I felt that I was making an important public statement: It was time to start fighting back and to put a stake in the ground declaring that *'as for me and my house-hold, we will serve the Lord'*.[12] I guess that was the start of a path-way along which we learnt to praise and worship God through our pain and our tears. In the Psalms and in the Church today there is much exuberance in worship and rightly so, because of God's great gift to us in Jesus but there are other expressions of worship too. The Bible speaks of the *'sacrifice of praise'*[13] and there are times in life such as the phase we were starting out on with Joshua, where worship is out of brokenness. But isn't that the heart of worship, whether we are jubilant or troubled? Worship remains an act on our part of abandoning ourselves in giving to Him who has given so much for us, whatever state we find ourselves in. The Bible talks about worshipping God *'in Spirit and in Truth'*.[14] We can worship anything and anyone, but godly worship requires us to get our focus right: onto Him. The truth about God, His character, His love for us, does not change.

---

[12] *Joshua 24 v 15* [13] *Psalm 107 v 22: 'Let them sacrifice thank offerings and tell of his works with songs of joy.' Hebrews 13 v 15-16: 'Through Jesus therefore, let us continually offer to God a sacrifice of praise - the fruit of lips that confess his name. And do not forget to do good and to share with others, for with such sacrifices God is pleased.'* [14] *John 4 v 24: 'God is spirit, and and his worshippers must worship in spirit and in truth.'*

This makes our worship of the Lord entirely independent of our circumstance, our moods and our situation - all of which change frequently. It is easier to praise God when things are going well for us, but it is also essential to worship Him when they are not. It became my lifeline in the hard times, bringing oxygen to my soul and spirit.

Chapter Four:

Roller-coasting for life

Coral Recounts

At last, Doctor Harper, our GOS consultant, explained to us that although unusually lumpy, Joshua had a very rare type of birthmark (called a melanocytic naevus) which would eventually grow hair and become like a giant mole. Even though there were so many separate marks from head to toe, it was all part of the same naevus, which was caused by an over-development of pigmented cells as the skin formed in the foetus. It would have happened very early in pregnancy, perhaps around the 5th week - this was further suggested because the mole tissue reached the extremities of his feet and hands, including some toes and fingers. It was nobody's fault but was so extremely rare that no one knew what had caused it.

'You need to prepare yourselves for a long haul of much hospitalisation in the coming years but I don't think you need to worry too much. He's very strong isn't he?' continued Doctor Harper. 'I want to remove some more lumps for analysis though. Can we operate tomorrow?'

It was such a relief that here was someone treating us seriously in our concerns for our baby and that he seemed utterly confident in what he was doing. Tim and I were both grateful to be admitted to such a prestigious hospital but at the same time it was quite a culture shock. Seeing the other children with obvious deformities we had never seen before was very disturbing and emotionally draining; such suffering and such abnormalities mixed with the remarkable resilience and acceptance of the children themselves. As we put our trust in the very capable doctors there, we suddenly realised the extent of our exhaustion.

Little sleep was managed that night on the ward before Joshua's first anaesthetic was administered early the next morning. A nice touch at GOS is that one parent stays with the child in the anaesthetic room until they have gone under. So Tim took our little bundle down. It was very hard to think of our week-old vulnerable baby having to go under the surgeon's knife - a procedure that even many adults escape in a lifetime. At the same time, it was reassuring that positive steps were being taken to understand fully the extent of Joshua's condition.

After a few hours, we started to become anxious that it was taking longer than planned. Then, rather than Joshua being returned to us as expected, we were confronted with anaesthetists and our doctor explaining that there had been a 'complication':

'The biopsies have been performed successfully, but during the procedure, Joshua vomited and has unfortunately inhaled it. Part of his lung has collapsed. He needs to be in Intensive Care to help him recover.'

'But I starved him as directed,' I protested. 'Why did it happen?'

'It's just one of those unfortunate things. It's the main risk of any anaesthetic and sometimes it just happens.'

As Joshua had only been out of the Special Care unit one night, the Intensive Care Unit (ICU) did not present such a scary concept and we were pacified surprisingly easily by the doctors' words that our baby should be fine in a few more days. It just meant we would be staying in the hospital a little longer.

In our state of shock still from his birth, this news was another thump in the stomach. The preceding week had been like a downward ride on a giant roller coaster; just as we thought we had reached the bottom and we thought we couldn't go any further down, we lunged downwards again. We felt numb.

As we were reunited with our baby again in ICU, we consoled ourselves that it couldn't get any worse. Several months later we learnt to stop using that phrase! It could and often it did - it's all a matter of perspective and how we react when it does. Our little infant seemed swamped by all the monitors and tubes and the little oxygen box over his head. It was a disturbing sight but comforting to watch his steady recovery. After only three days our little fighter no longer needed such intensive nursing and was moved to another cot on ICU. Sleeping down on the ward, Tim and I were getting used to our new residence and were biding our time until the biopsy results would be known. It was by no means an easy week.

While Joshua was in hospital, Doctor Harper took the opportunity to give him a more thorough checking over. Chest X-rays and ultrasounds of all his abdominal organs were performed and all appeared normal. Tim was fascinated to see all this and told me proudly that one of Joshua's kidneys was 37mm long, one millimetre per week of gestation! Why hadn't he gone into medicine?! All the activity was immensely reassuring for us, especially as the hospital policy ensured that as parents, we were fully involved and told the results as soon as the doctors knew them. It was a refreshing contrast to our experience of hospitals up to that point.

On the day of the biopsy results, it suddenly dawned on me that our boy was being tested for cancer. Why it took this long to sink in I do not know, other than that I was somehow protected from such a worry by my ignorance.

'Did you realise, Tim?' I questioned, to which he confessed that he had known of the potential since seeing a medical book in Barking Hospital. Another thump in the stomach as the roller coaster took another downward lunge. Within a couple of hours of piecing this together however, we were told that there was no 'frank malignancy' but the cells were nevertheless 'unusually active' and a close eye would need to be kept on them. Doctor Harper reiterated that it was virtually unheard of for cancer to develop in an unborn child but he did not fully understand all that was happening with Joshua. We appreciated his candour. It inspired our confidence in him.

Then it was time to take our son home at last. The consultant wanted to see us again in about a month, as he wanted to do further tests to check how deep the naevus went and establish whether his nervous system was affected. We were left with a feeling of total uncertainty concerning the future. It overshadowed everything. We would not even know whether our son was brain damaged by his condition until the next set of tests were performed.

Overall, we were both glad to come home but it was not the normal homecoming experience of most first time parents. We were frightened that the protection of having medical staff close at hand was no longer available to us. Our new responsibility made us somewhat nervous. As well as teddies and balloons, the nursery immediately filled with bandages and sterile equipment as the sores on Joshua's back needed cleaning and dressing twice a day. Amazingly the ulcer had not become infected but it still needed to be covered with sticky dressings and a 'boob tube' of gauze. In hospital he had worn no clothes at all but now in mid January at home he certainly needed them and it was a difficult and unhappy operation to dress and undress him. The sores on Joshua's neck were the most difficult as it was impossible to get dressings to stay in place there. Even at this tiny age he was very active and always moving his head around so it was inevitable that all his clothes were bloodstained around the collar. I always wanted to hide this from visitors as it looked so unsightly but it was not possible and I just had to live with it. Tim, however, wanted to show friends and relatives the unusual nature of Joshua's skin. He was much more 'matter of fact' about it than I and seemed driven to accept the skin condition. All my instincts were to make him look 'normal'. I was struggling with the idea of everyone seeing the ugliness of his condition. Deep down I was afraid that they would see my baby as ugly too and not just his skin.

During that time at home we noticed the lumps on Joshua's neck and back were growing more than he was and we were becoming increasingly concerned. He screamed at every nappy change and absolutely hated to lie on his back. It wasn't just existing lumps that were growing. New lumps were also appearing out of flat skin. By way of example, a new lump the size of a man's thumbnail grew up from nothing over 48 hours. Most of this active tissue was around the upper back and neck area. It was difficult to believe what we were seeing. 'Oh God help us and our boy' became an all too frequent prayer.

God answered this prayer in a way that we did not understand at the time, but it proved to be very significant. A pastor and his wife from California were visiting our pastors John and Dawn and they paid us a visit.

Everyone at church knew Dave Cunningham. He was the visiting speaker who came from time to time and always amazed us with his 'prophecies'. Many of our friends had been 'singled out' in a church meeting by Dave, who would pray for them and in front of everyone, tell them things about their lives which he could not possibly know, without God having somehow revealed it to him. We often found ourselves nodding in agreement and full of awe as he would go on to encourage these friends with what he felt God was saying to them personally. There were a few visiting speakers who had displayed this gift in our meetings but we had actually seen the results of our friends' lives changing after Dave had prayed in this way. It was dramatic and exciting whenever he came. So we respected Dave and his wife Vivien and felt it an honour that they should come to our house to pray with us.

In the process of the prayer, Dave sensed a clarity about Joshua's spirit and commented on his wonderful eyes, but told us we should start praying for the purity of Joshua's blood. This seemed a somewhat zany thing to pray for at the time. After all, his 'insides' were fine, it was only birthmarks and the skin on the outside which were the problem. But being obedient to this instruction and, for want of any other direction in which to pray specifically, we started praying that God would keep Joshua's blood pure and made it a regular prayer. We shared this prayer direction with our church and in time with other churches too. In the months and years to come the validity of this direction in prayer made it clear that God was involved in the detail of Joshua's care from the outset.

As so many people joined the network of those praying for us there was a demand for more information, and the telephone calls from our friends and family became hard to manage. We found ourselves writing a newsletter roughly once a month. Then as our story spread, the mailing list grew constantly throughout Joshua's life. The 'Joshua letters' were sent (and passed on) across the UK, Europe, the USA and Canada, Africa, the Caribbean and latterly Australia. Not many continents were left out! Our little son's progress was being followed by a great number of people. To give some examples of this, a friend of Tim's sister was telling his wife the latest news on Joshua in his shop in Bournemouth, but hadn't used Joshua's name. A customer in the shop overheard and cut in with, 'Are you talking about baby Joshua in London? My prayer group is praying for him.'

Similarly, friends of ours with a beauty salon a number of miles away from us had a similar experience and it made us feel very humble that so many people were interested and were petitioning God for us. At the same time it was very reassuring to receive occasional letters back and to know that so much prayer was going on.

Just before our boy was five weeks old, we were so concerned about the ever-growing lumps that we telephoned GOS and got a surprisingly fast appointment the next day. Before we knew what was happening, we were admitted again for further tests. We were learning to live 'one day at a time', not knowing whether we would even be sleeping at home or in hospital but that not being our greatest concern anymore; we were beginning to understand exactly why the Bible teaches us to live like that anyway.[15]

---

[15] *Matthew 6 v 34: 'Therefore, do not worry about tomorrow, for tomorrow will worry about itself. Each day has enough trouble of its own.'*

By this stage, friends and family were beginning to say that they didn't know how we were coping. We would reply that it was down to God's help and grace alone and, looking back, that fact is even more clear to us. After a matter of time we got more used to not looking ahead for more than a few days or weeks maximum, but initially it was hard not to. During this phase, our friend Richard Griffin brought a particularly useful illustration to us:

'When you focus on today, you see today's problems and issues, but you are experiencing them alongside today's provision of God's grace for you, so you are able to see them as God sees them and cope. When you look ahead, the danger is that you will see the problems, but will not be able to anticipate the help that God will give you at that time to handle them. God's grace will only be given at the time that it is needed.'

It was very easy to get overwhelmed by the uncertainty of the future, so as we experienced more and more of God's help and presence with us in the present, we grew in confidence that God would be with us whatever we had to face in the future too.

Back on the ward for the second time, the hospital felt more familiar and almost homely. We were excited to learn a little more about potential cosmetic surgery techniques which would help improve our son's appearance but there was frustratingly little information about his condition and controversy over the benefits of the treatment available. Our optimism for the cosmetic work was soon dented when the top surgeon refused to take Joshua on.

'His skin is so poor it will never heal, so surgery is contra-indicated,' was his parting comment. By the next day however, Doctor Harper, whom we were beginning to recognise as very influential in the hospital, had found a Senior Registrar on the plastic surgery team who was prepared to take Joshua on. This both excited us and filled us with trepidation. For me, the drive to get my son cosmetically perfect was all consuming. Tim was much more thoughtful and did not want Joshua to be put at undue risk. In the end we agreed that the surgeon, Mr. Foley, should take a further four biopsies and perform just a test patch 'dermabrasion'[16] at the same time.

Over the next ten days in hospital other tests were performed to check his eyes, liver, kidneys, lungs and, because he had also started projectile vomiting at home, even his stomach was investigated. We were relieved when all came out clear. At this time, we also learnt that the birthmarks stopped just short of affecting his nervous system, as confirmed by his lively interaction with us. We still needed all the reassuring news we could get and we were thankful to God that our son was not brain damaged.

Then came the distressing part. At only six weeks old it was confirmed that two of the four biopsies were showing malignant melanoma and it was therefore concluded that he had been carrying this most dangerous and rare form of skin cancer since birth after all.

The oncology consultant, Doctor Pritchard, was brought in to break the news, which devastated us both. No matter how hard I tried, I could not stop the tears spilling out as he explained the seriousness of this new finding as kindly as he could. Somehow, Tim had been expecting it all along but to me it was a sudden death sentence, which was sounding harshly certain. As Joshua was only one of around six babies world-wide known to be born

---

[16] '*dermabrasion*" *was the plastic surgery technique to be used which involved shaving the top layer of birthmarked skin, with a view to it growing back a paler colour.*

with malignant melanoma, a prognosis was extremely hard. The only thing known for certain about melanoma was and is, its unpredictable nature but still, phone calls would be made to other hospitals including one in Scotland, another in Memphis USA and one in Paris, in an attempt to find other case histories that might help. Ordinarily melanoma is caused by over-exposure to the sun and although this is often through burns in childhood, it is usually much later in life that it manifests itself. Doctor Pritchard had only seen about ten cases of melanoma in children in twenty years of specialising in children's' rare cancers. The usual treatment would be total surgical removal of both the offending malignant mole and also a fairly wide margin of normal skin around it but in Joshua's case this simply was not possible due to the widespread area of mole tissue which entirely covered his neck and back. There was too much for surgery alone to stand a chance of curing him. We both reeled from shock. With all this explanation, Doctor Pritchard was careful to emphasise how grim the situation was looking and it was almost too much to take in.

When pushed, Doctor Pritchard gave an estimated life expectancy of four to six months. Once more, we felt winded. Just when we had come to terms with the latest circumstance or disappointment and had proven yet again God's sufficiency to sustain us, the spiral of events would thrust us yet further downwards. As we were pushed to the limits emotionally and medically, the only resource that proved to be limitless to us was God's strength. We were numb and stripped bare. It was like when someone dies and it is hard to believe what you are hearing, yet at the same time you know you have to hear the truth and in as much detail as possible. I realised that I was in shock at that moment but I still had to listen very carefully. I felt bloated with all the information I had already taken in but still I wanted more. What was going to happen now? Perhaps there was a chance hiding somewhere in all the fog? If so, what did it look like? I just could not accept that Joshua would be dead in six months and I was searching for something positive to cling to.

The only possible option seemed to be a course of some kind of chemotherapy although this was rarely very effective with melanoma. We were advised to start considering if it was what we wanted. But at the same time we were also aware that it is God who gives and takes life and that doctors neither have all the answers nor are they holding all the cards. Tim suddenly reminded me of the prophetic advice Dave Cunningham had brought us about praying for the purity of his blood and incredibly it now made total sense. For the cancer to spread it must travel through the blood system, so if that stays pure, the cancer can go no further than his skin. We were very excited by this, especially as we had been praying that way even before the cancer was diagnosed. At the same time it caused us to feel very humble that God would have set us on the right course in prayer even before we knew what we were up against. It showed us something of His parenting of us that He should prepare us in that way and at least in part, it eased the pain of what we were facing.

We felt alone and even isolated by the uniqueness of our circumstance, but the rarity of Joshua's condition made us love him all the more. As we fell in love with our unique little son we were conscious of the vulnerability in love, that he may well die, leaving us with greater pain commensurate with the depth of our feeling for him. Yet to protect ourselves by closing off from him emotionally was abhorrent and would have been selfish. Love and acceptance were the two qualities he needed most and it seemed these at least were fully within our power to give or to withhold against the general backdrop of helplessness. We were also conscious of our need to stay close with God continually and to ask for His view on things. During this time the story of Abraham offering up his son Isaac made a lot of sense to us. Our natural instincts as fledgling parents were to hold on to Joshua as tightly as possible. Yet this Old Testament example seemed to suggest that, even though children are a gift from God, we should live in ultimate surrender of them to His will. This was a hard struggle. Could we honestly say to God: 'It's Your prerogative to let Joshua live or die. We entrust his future to You, whatever the outcome'? The process was a powerful one, as it taught us to live out God's sovereign right to rule in our lives, attitudes and circumstances. This became the theme of Joshua's dedication service held at church on Sunday 21st March. What we discovered was that great peace and security followed, having surrendered Joshua to God.

After the doctors' research was completed there was still very little experience of Joshua's condition. A course of chemotherapy was devised and with much heart-searching we agreed to a six-week trial period. We would at least see if it was working or not from the very visible response in his skin. First of all though the surgeon would try to remove as much tumour as possible.

It was an amazing operation on 23rd March. Two and a half hours of brilliant surgery by the American Mr. Foley totally transformed Joshua's back to be almost completely flat for the first time in his two and a half months of life. Debulking the tumours in this way would give the chemo less disease to work on as well as making our boy more comfortable. He had more

stitching than his clothing by the end of it but, despite the doctors' earlier concerns, he healed quickly and beautifully to everyone's delight. It had been four weeks exactly since his previous
surgery. The next day he was to be seen sitting in his bouncy
chair as if nothing had happened! As this was contrary to all the
doctors' expectations we thanked God for His answer to our
prayers and felt genuinely high.

His excellent response to surgery became a pattern which we
believe was evidence of God answering the prayers of many people world-wide as, according to one of the leading British paediatric consultant surgeons at least, Joshua's skin was likely to
ulcerate and should not have tolerated surgery so well! Joshua
went on to have over thirty operations, each healing beautifully
every time. Many things in Joshua's life remain inexplicable if we
remove the belief in the direct intervention of God from the
equation. We came to depend on God's intervention in answer
to the prayers of many people and churches around the world.

Cancer and chemotherapy are two words that evoke a common reaction of dread from many. Add a baby or even a child to
that combination and the cocktail is the more potent in its emotional effect. Entering the Oncology ward for the first time with
our three-month-old was a sickening experience. The seriousness of the plight of the many children staying on the ward per-
meated the atmosphere as did the anxiety of the parents. Yet
amidst it all, the brave resilience of the patients themselves shone
through. Up until this point Joshua had been growing stronger
and stronger, thriving on a diet of his mum's breast milk and
anaesthesia! We were dreading the effect the chemotherapy
might bring to pull this down, but at first it went surprisingly
well. If anything, Joshua tolerated his chemo better than us! He

kept his hair, continued to feed and grow well and only once had
a slight 'blip' when he needed blood because his red count
dropped below a tolerable level. Even then it was only noticed
by the daily blood tests and he certainly did not appear ill affected. It was a worrying time for us though. We were very unused
to the 'Hickman Line' catheter and the sterile dressings and procedures they required and we kept expecting something dreadful
to happen. Most of all was the fear of the unknown. There were
still so many unanswered questions. 'Would Joshua live? Were
we doing the right thing with the chemo? What had caused his
condition? Would future children be born with the same thing?
What if he died?' There was so much that we didn't know and
we were often perplexed and confused.

After the week of drugs we were allowed home. This time we
were armed with a dustbin bag full of medical supplies to add to
the already burgeoning pharmacy in Joshua's nursery! The plan
was set up for us to continue with the second course of
chemotherapy at our local hospital, due in about a week after
getting home. But before we got that far, Joshua decided he had
had enough of this wiggly line and pulled it clean out of his chest
one night! As we dried him after his bath I suddenly noticed a
gaping red hole where the line should have been, at the same split
second as Tim picked up a length of white silicone tubing from
the carpet! A quick phone call to GOS informed us that there
was a small chance that Joshua may be haemorrhaging internally.
He would need to be checked and as time was of the essence, we
should take him to the local hospital. We bundled him into the
car in a state of near panic.

Arriving at about 9 p.m. with Joshua in one arm and his
Hickman Line in the other, we half ran straight to the children's

ward, but it seemed to take forever while a doctor was bleeped and finally arrived. His first question was 'What's a Hickman Line? I've never seen one of them before!' Tim dangled Joshua's line under the doctor's nose and explained that this one end should still be passing through Joshua's main vein and dangling in the right atrium of his heart, whilst this other end should be protruding from Joshua's chest, for the administration of drugs such as certain chemotherapy.

'And by the way,' he added with restrained anger, 'Don't you think you should be checking to see whether he is haemorrhaging internally?'

'Oh, I'll send a nurse in,' the doctor replied.

Many questions followed, as the doctor had never seen anything like Joshua's condition. Rationally, we knew we could not expect local staff to have seen it, but the strain of feeling you knew more than they did was exhausting.

Receiving chemo at the local hospital did not go well, especially when the same doctor who had never seen a Hickman Line before walked in with the first dose. We were not surprised when Joshua developed a line infection in his new line. As a result, we were then admitted there and suffered yet more traumas. Compared with GOS, the cubicle was even smaller and the sound of babies and children crying for their mummies was incessant throughout the day and night. It was almost impossible to sleep. Exhaustion and depression like never before came on me and worst of all, our bright-eyed, energetic, 'living and loving life to the full' baby was becoming ill, perhaps never to recover.

Again, God knew what we needed and when we needed it. As we rushed home several days later to collect a few things, with me in floods of tears from the strain of it all, John and Dawn brought round another pastor and his wife to pray with us. Peter and Brenda Parris were also from the States and Peter, an excellent Bible teacher, often spoke at our church. His wife Brenda had just been diagnosed with breast cancer and they both empathised so much with us. By this time I was becoming very used to crying before people I did not know. As they prayed, God replenished us and we felt instantly stronger.

When we chatted afterwards, God gave us another important piece of strategy on how to respond correctly to Joshua's condition. Brenda felt that in her own battle with cancer, God had shown her how to deal with the fear of it. The Bible teaches us that we should fear nothing other than God Himself.[17] Something was sparked in us and from that point on we also lost our fear of the 'Big C'.

Meanwhile, Joshua's fever would not be calmed with anything. The vomiting started in earnest again and he was losing weight. Maybe that could have been put down to the chemotherapy but the little man got no better when the chemo and antibiotics ended and we should have been taking him home. We felt that we needed the reassurance of the specialists again, so we grabbed the first opportunity to transfer him back to GOS ourselves. I believe we got him into London just in time, as it looked like we were certainly losing him. Our little boy was ashen-faced and delirious as his temperature bounced around 106°F. We had never seen him this bad and GOS quickly diagnosed septicaemia. It was also discovered that there was now a trace of infection on his lungs.

---

[17] *Isaiah 8 v 12, 13; Romans 8 v15; Revelation 2 v 10*

Back home at our church, everyone was praying for Joshua and we heard of prayer meetings, which were more passionate and better attended than the church had seen before. There was fasting and intense times of really seeking God - times when they too felt the very presence of God among them. It was very humbling to know so much attention was being directed towards us again and that the Lord was using it to bless our friends in their praying. We heard that people were getting really excited about praying and some usually quiet members of the church were finding new freedom in expression. Any inhibitions seemed suddenly rather futile. Even more amazing to us was that this same reaction was repeated across many congregations in churches throughout the UK and across the world. Although we didn't realise it at the time, there was clearly something very special in the depth of response Joshua's plight evoked in complete strangers. The story was always the same; it seemed whoever so much as heard about Joshua found themselves drawing together with other Christians in passionate prayer for him.

After ten days of Joshua's condition worsening, it became clear that the only option was to take out the Hickman Line. This would mean that no further chemotherapy could be administered but as the cancer had continued to grow through the treatment anyway, there was little point. Within two days of removing this second line (and of course using the opportunity for yet another biopsy), Joshua then made a remarkable recovery; which was something he became expert at. We were even allowed home for a short while again. In five short but dramatic months, all conventional treatments for our son's cancer had been tried and failed. We were now entering the uncharted waters of experimental treatments. We had not anticipated parenthood being like this. Without God's help the future looked bleak and uncertain.

Chapter Five:

This happened so that the work of God might be displayed

Coral Recounts

Already emerging was the delightful character of a child who loved nothing more than to be passed from person to person, treating each one to smiles before wriggling off for the next bit of action. Joshua's love of people was insatiable and he never tired of new faces. I found that the only sure way to pacify his noisier moments (and there were plenty of them!) was to hold him tight against my body and do deep squats to the floor over and over again. It seemed he had also inherited my love for aerobics and many nurses learnt this with the result that they had aching legs! Tim went as far as vowing to ban me from exercise if I ever fell pregnant again. His knees and thigh muscles would not sustain such exertions again he claimed and he often tried to pass Joshua back to me for pacifying, claiming that it was my fault for doing such vigorous exercise at seven months pregnant in the first place!

We were as keen as the doctors to crack on with treatment, so when we found ourselves back in hospital only six days after the chemotherapy stopped, we were not displeased. A harrowing two weeks ensued while Joshua's body adjusted to his new 'experimental' medication - alpha-interferon. Then we were allowed home again, but home for what?

'If only we knew if he is going to live or die,' we frequently reasoned, 'we could then adjust ourselves emotionally. If only we knew which it would be, it would be easier to handle.' We were in grief and joy, pain and expectancy. Both sets of emotions jarred and sparred with one another daily. There was the grief and pain of seeing how precarious our baby Joshua's health and life were and how much medical intervention he was enduring. The very real possibility that this could end in death at any time was set against the joy and delight at the emergent strong personality, the sparkling eyes and oblivion to his unusual life revolving around surgery, anaesthesia and toxic drugs. His joy and acceptance of the abnormal filled us with pride. As first time parents we also started to experience the emotional charge of the wonder of new life, the instinctive hopes and dreams for the child and his future. But like a battering ram, they hit the wall of 'will he live?'

We even started to ask the big 'Why?' question. The medics checked out our family medical histories, as part of their research into naevus babies, but well-meaning people had also hinted to us about our 'spiritual' histories - perhaps there were skeletons in our pasts which had led to God allowing Joshua to be born like this. After all, there are biblical references to 'punishing the children for the sins of the fathers...'.[18] In me, this sense of potential guilt was no more than a transitory reaction: 'Did I do something dangerous in pregnancy?' I wondered, quickly dismissing the idea as there was nothing to think of. For Tim, the same questioning reaction was less conscious and more

---

[18] *Deuteronomy 5 v 9: For I the Lord your God, am a jealous God, punishing the children for the sin of the fathers to the third and fourth generation of those who hate me.*

irrational. Unwittingly, guilt became a weight on Tim's shoulders. He now reached one of his lowest moments so far and that had a devastating effect on both of us.

We took a much-needed holiday by visiting Tim's sister and family in Bournemouth and on our last day there, Tim's brother Phil also joined us. In the evening, we found ourselves all together having an impromptu time praying for Joshua's healing. We wanted to know what God was saying. It was one of those times when we realised how much we needed God to intervene and speak to us - and that we couldn't go on without knowing something fresh from Him. It is after all a biblical promise that His mercies are new every morning and that yesterday's 'manna' is no good for today. Then Phil told us he had felt directed by God to share the story of John 9 with us. It is where Jesus heals a blind man by spitting on some mud and rubbing it on his eyes. 'Uh oh' I thought, 'what's coming next? A mud pack for our baby?' However, Phil felt that the relevance to Joshua was in the conversation that followed between Jesus and his disciples:

> *As he [Jesus] went along, he saw a man blind from birth. His disciples asked him, 'Rabbi, who sinned, this man or his parents, that he was born blind?' 'Neither this man nor his parents sinned,' said Jesus, 'but this happened so that the work of God might be displayed in his life.'*[19]

It was surely God speaking to us again because Phil had not been aware that we had even begun the dreaded 'Why?' question. The weight lifted from Tim's shoulders at the same time, as he became conscious that he had been worrying about why it had

---

[19] *John 9 v 1-7*

happened. The guilt dispersed and I was grateful to see his mood lighten. Even more encouraging was the idea that Joshua had been born so that God's glory would somehow be revealed through his life. There was no direct answer as to whether Joshua would continue to live or die, but suddenly the question lost its immediate importance to us because here was God telling us that, whatever happened, Joshua's life would bring glory to Him and we knew it rang true. Already he had brought people together in prayer like never before (not least ourselves) and this was just a small indication to us that God was really going to use Joshua's life powerfully and for good.

So we left Bournemouth on our way up the roller-coaster for once and went on to enjoy a further recuperative break in the quietness of Llanelli, South Wales with very good friends. Even the sun came out for us that week, although we had to be scrupulous about keeping Joshua protected from its harmful rays.

Back home we started to unpack - an activity we were becoming all too familiar with, when as usual the phone started ringing. It was one of our church elders, Loxley Ford, with news that he had received a call from war-torn Sierra Leone where a small fellowship of Christians was praying for Joshua. It was amazing to think they could even think about our son when we knew these people had been fleeing their homes in fear for their lives at that time. Not long before Joshua was born, our church had been praying for their pastor Richard Cole who was literally hiding in a cave in the mountains while rebel fighters were threatening his family. So it was astounding that this man was now calling us with the encouragement of a Bible passage he felt the Lord wanted us to know concerning Joshua. As soon as Loxley told me the Bible reference, it was too exciting to even listen to the rest of what he had to say! It was John 9 again, emphasising to us that it was no one's fault, but rather this had happened so that the work of God would be revealed through Joshua's life!

Imagine the scene when, the following day, Loxley telephoned again because he had received another call from Brenda Parris in America. She had also been praying for Joshua and wanted to pass on John 9 to us. We were truly elated. It was so wonderful but it did not end there. As we shared these stories with our friends and family, we learnt that the same passage had been brought to the minds of at least two others when Joshua was first born. We were in no doubt that God wanted to encourage us with those particular words and even that we should use them now as a direction for prayer. We made sure that the people all over the world who were already praying for us could also be encouraged by and use this scripture. Again and again, when we did not know what to pray any more, the Holy Spirit reminded us to pray that the Glory of God would be seen in Joshua's life. God changed our hearts and the desire to see the fulfilment of this scripture became foundational to us. The desire to know whether he would live or die paled into insignificance now that God had reassured us that all this was for a purpose – for His glory to be revealed through Joshua's life.

From late May I was treated to the delightful feeling that we had finally come home, with our son having reached the age of five months! Every two weeks saw us driving up to the Outpatients clinic at GOS but these check-ups were going well, as the growth in lumps seemed to be abating at last. Joshua continued to develop well. He was very much a 'party animal' who demanded to be the centre of attention. The more noise and activity the better and he would soon complain if it were too quiet or he had stayed in the same room for too long - five minutes was considered too long for him! Because he was not yet mobile, he had his own way of letting you know he wanted to be carried all the time and a babywalker became my lifesaver. At last he could whizz around the house in any direction as fast as he liked and the happiness it gave him was well worth the chipped paintwork and bruised ankles! He became inseparable from his 'wheels' and we found ourselves taking them everywhere. He had such an active personality that he was exhausting just to watch, but I was reassured by all this energy and would not have changed him, even if I could.

The hardest thing that first summer was getting used to other people staring at Joshua or making thoughtless comments. Even the natural curiosity of children, who would do double-takes as they walked past in the street or remark loudly in the supermarket, was really hurting me. I would hear things like: 'Look at that baby, look at all those spots mummy,' and I wanted to slap down every pointing finger or deliberately shock these 'ignorant' people by telling them he had cancer so they would then feel guilty. Nevertheless, in discussing this with our pastor John and his wife Dawn, I knew I had a wrong attitude and was going down a route to anger and bitterness. Usually all they had done was to question whether Joshua had chicken pox or to ask what had happened to him. Perhaps I felt that I was being accused of something by such a question as that one often riled me the most. I found myself delivering a somewhat curt reply of, 'Nothing!' followed by a silent, 'and it's none of your business!' My own anger was the problem. After all, it was unlikely that the situation would change and I knew it would do Joshua no good to learn from a mother who was always furious with the world.

He too would have to learn how to deal with peoples' reactions and his response would be a crucial part of his development in years to come. So, although my reactions were perfectly understandable and even quite easy to defend, it was not healthy for me to carry on like this and I knew it. First I had to repent and then, with God's help, I could begin to make the adjustment for Joshua's sake as well as my own.

I fought off the other instincts I had to cover my baby in public or hide him in the house all day. That was almost impossible anyway with such a demanding, outgoing child. I reasoned that perhaps if I took him out locally often enough people would eventually get used to him and certainly he soon became well known in the community as I walked him out in the buggy two or three times a day. I was still caught off guard sometimes with the questioning and each time I came to ask God's forgiveness until I found my anger subsiding. Then I started diffusing situations before they happened by opening the conversation and this prevented many awkward stares as well as preventing people from making mistakes and feeling even more embarrassed. It made me more outgoing in the end, as I had to make the first move in talking to almost everyone I met.

By this time I had used all my maternity leave from my banking job and even a further extension period granted in consideration of my special circumstances. But I could not, nor did I have the desire to, return to work full time. I was grateful that my special circumstances provoked sufficient compassion from my employers for them to create a short-term, part-time position. Having explained about frequent hospitalisation at a moment's notice, they were very understanding and a position was created which allowed me flexible working from home with only one monthly meeting in the office. Most of this I could organise around Joshua's sleep time, but I expanded it to about twelve hours a week by leaving him with my friend Amanda Simmons for one or two afternoons. With two slightly older boys, Amanda had plenty of experience and all the appropriate toys with which to keep our Joshy amused. She never admitted until later how much harder he was to entertain than her own two, Jeremy and Toby and how the latter were employed to set off every musical toy or noisy item to amuse my son whenever he came! Apparently they always knew when Joshua had 'been to play' because every toy was strewn across the carpet and each one was wet from his eager chewing.

Meanwhile, the daily interferon injections were going well, with no side-effects that we noticed and it was not uncommon for me to manage to inject him single-handed and without tears. It was so much preferable to our most hated Hickman Line and all the sterile paraphernalia that accompanied it. Even the hospital clinic appointments dropped to six weekly for checking Joshua's internal organs. The cancer was still sitting there in his skin, but incredibly, not spreading. We continued to pray for the purity of Joshua's blood and even the lumps in his skin seemed to stop growing or bleeding

Joshua was doing so well that it was agreed to attempt some cosmetic/preventative surgery along with the next biopsies and I was excited by this idea. I was almost looking forward to operations in the way that most people anticipate their summer holidays or an expensive haircut. It was always the next thing to focus upon. It was always a few weeks into the future and it gave the hope of a slightly improved life afterwards! Each surgery now meant less bleeding tumour and potentially less birthmark, so I was usually counting the days and was fully prepared to accept the short-term discomfort and concern for him that each admission brought. Or at least, I always thought this to be so until we got there!

The night before going back into GOS, the worries would drift in and there would be the inevitable upset stomach to remind me I was stressed after all. Seeing my baby son's pain at the hands of hospital procedures, I longed to do the hurting for him. Any parent would want to do this rather than stand by and watch their child suffer. So when it came to the pre-operative anxiety, I was glad that this was one bit of 'suffering' I could do for Joshua. It was nothing compared to what he had to endure but time and again I thanked God that at least his tender age made him blissfully unaware of what was being planned and he was therefore unable to worry. As Tim carried Joshua into the anaesthesia room, the theatre nurse greeted them BOTH by name, causing Tim to reflect that they were indeed regular visitors to this part of the hospital, where patients are usually anonymous, unconscious beings ready to be operated on. Two days after this particular operation we were again heading for home with Joshua totally swathed in thick padded bandages from armpits to groin. He had recovered well and we were further encouraged by our consultant oncologist just prior to leaving. He could hardly believe that Joshua was still alive and now seven months old. He was delighted (although surprised) to bring the news that his internal organs were still perfectly clear.

As the cancer did not appear to be behaving 'normally', the oncologist then decided to widen the gap between check-ups even further. A plan was formulated to allow the surgeon to continue operating on the tumours and growths on the back of

Joshua's head, neck and shoulders, with a series of small operations as often as Joshua could tolerate them. According to his
recovery of late, this would probably mean an operation every six
to eight weeks and this was an incredibly positive step forward
for us. In reality, such plans always had a habit of changing so we
continued to live from one operation to the next.

The next date was early October and all was going to plan
with some sixteen lumps removed, including two hard, black,
marble-sized ones deep inside Joshua's neck. The surgeon
thought they might have been the source of the surface cancers.
Again Joshua returned from surgery, wide awake and kicking. It
seemed as though general anaesthetics were acting as a tonic to
him and he was so hyperactive that we had real trouble even getting him to sleep that night. By 11 p.m., his dad was hyper-
grumpy!

Eventually, we all settled down to sleep with Tim in Joshua's
cubicle and me up in the mum's dormitory. Tim got the raw deal
here because unfortunately at around 2 a.m. Joshua's temperature soared up to 107.6 degrees and the nurses were running
around getting intravenous drips and antibiotics set up for him.
It was a bad night and an even bigger surprise when another
twelve hours later, a blood test confirmed septicaemia once
again. This meant a different, stronger antibiotic, a drip and
painful blood tests. His temperature chart looked like a cross
section of the Alps, as the blood infection refused to be beaten.

After several days of this I was desperate. Being confined to
the tiny cubicle for such long days with a sick and unhappy baby
was not a pleasant experience. Tim was going to the office during the day, which was good distraction for him but I was getting
really downhearted. Why was this happening with all the prayer

going on around the world for Joshua? Why was God ignoring us all? It did not make any sense and to make matters worse, even when he did recover from this infection, it caused the doctors to rethink their strategy and postpone any future operation until January. He would be one by then and I was all too conscious that concerning the birthmarks, he looked little different from the day he was born despite his nine operations so far. People were often telling me how cute he was and I loved him to bits but as he was growing up, I was so concerned that 'Joe Public', who did not know him for his character, would not be so generous in reacting to Joshua's appearance.

Still the pain continued during that hospital stay. The line in Joshua's wrist, which had been inserted during the operation, was causing him to scream and scream every time it was used for drugs, until finally it had to come out and a new one was inserted in a different site. Well, this was almost too much to bear as the doctor tried time and again to get a needle into his tiny vein without collapsing it. Joshua was beside himself. Finally, after an hour, the anaesthetist was called to see if she would have any more success but even she failed and Joshua was left like a very bruised and upset pincushion, on top of his high temperature. Like so many of our experiences to date, this was the worst. There are simply not enough superlatives sometimes to describe the depth of despair a mother feels on watching her child's pain helplessly, while someone else inflicts it.

In the end there was nothing else to be done, Joshua had to have another operation to put a line into the big vein in his groin under anaesthetic. In little over a week I had sunk so low that I got to the point where I could not imagine ever taking Joshua home again happy and well. I had been reading my Bible daily at this point but just did not seem to be getting any answers. I happened to pick up a book, which was left by a visitor one evening and I started reading about prayer. What I read then hit me with real excitement in the midst of my anguish. I accepted it as a direct answer to my crying to God as I read again the story of Moses.[20] He was on a hilltop praying for his army with his arms stretched up to Heaven. He saw that if he lowered his arms, his army would start losing the fight and if he lifted them up again, his side would start winning. So he enlisted the help of his friends to hold his arms up for him when he was too tired to manage for himself. As I read this, I just knew that God was saying we had to keep praying for Joshua and if that praying eased off, there would be setbacks as there were in the battle Moses was praying for.

As I read on, I was reminded who the leader of Moses' army was - I was amazed that I had even missed his name when I first read it - and I even knew the story. It was the biblical Joshua! The reassurance I gained from this especially was that the whole story demonstrated the power of the prayer, not of Joshua himself, for he would have been too busy with the battle. It was effective for others to be doing the praying and necessary for friends to be involved in this too. It enabled me to accept that sometimes I was too tired to pray anymore myself but others were there to 'hold up my arms'.

When the biopsy results came through we were again pleased to learn that only two of the sixteen lumps removed were malignant. We were thrilled at such a positive result, as it seemed to indicate that the proportion of malignant lumps was reducing.

---

[20] *Exodus 17 v 10 - 13*

In the normal day to day things, feeding continued to be a problem and I used every distraction technique I could think of to keep this child happy in his high chair long enough to get sufficient food in. Eating itself was simply not exciting so I resorted to silly faces, animal sounds and peek-a-boo games in a mighty effort to keep him entertained. In this way, I could sneak in the spoonfuls although it would take up to an hour every meal. I wondered if other mums had to work so hard at meal times and I envied those who clearly did not.

Altogether, we would have said that we had a good summer, but small new lumps were still growing. We prayed hard for more surgery until on 4th November thirty-one lumps were removed for biopsy from the back of Joshua's head, neck, shoulders, back and sides. A week later, the enormous bandages were removed to reveal perfect healing and we looked forward to hearing the biopsy results once more.

The news was astounding. Among the thirty-one biopsies, the pathology report confirmed there was NO malignancy! Did this mean our surgeon had finished his 'curative' work already? After all, he had removed everything that looked vaguely cancerous. Did it mean Joshua was free of cancer? Our imaginations took flight as we remembered the deep tumours removed in the previous surgery, which, it was speculated, might have been the root of the surface cancers. But there were no definite answers. There was no way of escaping the threat which would always hang over Joshua's life and we had to be careful not to raise our hopes unduly, only to have them smashed again.

We were succeeding in enjoying our little man - now 'crawling' with his elbows like the little commando soldier he really was. There was so much character to this little lad that it was hard to believe he was not even a year old. He would look you in the eyes with such intensity, you could well believe he knew far more than he could ever communicate. He certainly treated everyone with a singular self-confidence and there was no denying the presence he had about him as he gave out his orders in words of one grunt.

Just before Christmas, our local paper got to hear about Joshua from one of the members of our church and approached us to do a seasonal 'good news' story for their front page. We remembered a girl from the north of England who had been to the States for pioneering surgery just at the time Joshua was born. Her parents had to use the media to get the necessary funds and at first they were treated sensitively. However, when everything went wrong for the little girl and she died, her parents were in the public gaze again. They were in the news daily throughout the first weeks of their grief and there was no way we wanted that type of pressure if it ever came to that, so we were somewhat hesitant at first. Still, eventually we were persuaded, and it was agreed that nothing should be given to the national press and we could even see the copy before they went to print.

'Thank God! - little Joshua - the baby who linked the world in prayer' read the headlines. It was a good article and we were not displeased with the way it was written, particularly as it acknowledged the significance of the power of God in Joshua's life. Our first encounter with the press also brought to us a sense of vulnerability. It was a real eye-opener as to how journalists work. What we thought was just a friendly conversation turned out to be an interview by phone and within seconds of answering a few questions, the journalist had woven an elaborate story out of a few brief answers. The power of the pen!

We felt out of our depth when we were approached by two of the national tabloid newspapers. One was easily put off by our local paper on our behalf. The other was a more insistent free-lance writer and we had to learn very quickly the rules of the game. In our naivety, we had believed we might have some control over any story written about our son and we continued to assert our wishes for anonymity. So we politely refused to answer the reporters' questions. We politely refused the request for pictures to be taken of him and we tried to decline to give a story. It turned out to be less easy than we imagined.

We had no idea of how persistent some of these people could be. Short of hanging up the telephone mid sentence, it was almost impossible to get them to leave us alone. All the assertive techniques taught to us on courses at our places of employment did not seem to be working and in the end they even tried emotional blackmail to get us to talk to them, before turning nasty.

'You have no control over your story, it's in the public domain. We don't even need your permission. We can print what we like' was the reporter's parting shot. Thankfully, in the event this did not happen. The whole thing left us feeling like a commodity for public consumption rather than human beings with the right to privacy and we had new sympathy and admiration for those frequently in the public gaze. It upset us and took the edge off an otherwise exciting 'first Christmas'.

Christmas was soon over and then came Joshua's birthday. Apart from the obvious birthmarks, he was thriving, so we decided to celebrate. Joshua always displayed fantastic energy and vitality even among children his own age. There was nothing quiet about him, no hint of shyness with anyone and definitely nothing subdued. So Joshua's first birthday party had to be along similar grandiose lines. We had to hire a hall for about 130 guests of all ages and we decided to combine extravagant cakes and a party atmosphere with a time of worship and thanks to God at the conclusion.

We decorated the hall with balloons and pictures and even put up a display of photographs of Joshua to show how his appearance had improved with age and cosmetic surgery. We produced a medical summary of all that he had undergone in twelve months and both wept and wondered at how much he had endured so valiantly. As usual, he careered about in his walker, 'chatting' to everyone in his unintelligible babble and thoroughly loving being the focus of so many people's attention. It was a truly wonderful day and we were so grateful to all our friends and family who came - particularly those who drove long distances. Dave Cunningham, the Californian pastor, also came along as he was in town that weekend. Not many one-year-olds have so many friends to invite and entertain and not many could have sustained the level of excitement Joshua did throughout the day. It was definitely a high point for us.

The day we thought he would never see proved to be a tremendous milestone for us all and for once we put our concerns about the future to one side and just thanked God that he had made it this far.

Chapter Six:
Today I held a miracle
Coral Recounts

T wo days after Joshua's party we were back in hospital again. By this time he had had nearly 100 lumps removed, although the exact number was beginning to blur and even the surgeon was giving up on counting them. We had also spent a total of thirteen weeks as in-patients at GOS by the time Joshua was one year old!

A new wing had just opened and we all enjoyed the facilities that came with staying there. What luxury we had now, with our own en suite bathroom and a cubicle big enough for us all to sleep in. This was 'Tiger' ward and all our nurse friends were there to greet us and make a fuss of the growing Joshua. The boy himself was visibly excited by his bright new surroundings and places to explore. He loved the murals depicting jungle scenes and it was a fun coincidence that tigers were his favourite animals - one of only two he could mimic. Dogs and cats were too tame for this little soldier; he imitated tigers and snakes instead! Joshy's strong personality won him a place in hearts everywhere.

Television cameras were on the ward too as the BBC was doing a special programme on another patient on our ward. Joshua was filmed playing with a delightful eight-year-old. Each morning she would do her own 'doctor's round' and check on each patient on the ward. She was another of GOS's 'veterans' who had survived many a scare against the odds and was now doing well - hence the documentary film. Joshua warmed to her as he did to everyone who paid him attention and it was heart-breaking when her operation went tragically wrong the next day with fatal consequences. The intensity of the grief and anger that arose in us came as a surprise because we had hardly known the family.

We found ourselves more worried for this little girl's parents than we were for ourselves, realising that we were experiencing the grace of God to help us cope with Joshua. We were right in the situation rather than looking on, so we HAD to look to God for His help to keep us sane. Without experiencing God there is only anxiety and despair at the circumstances of suffering - especially child death. As onlookers to this family, we could not see how the Lord might be helping them and it was particularly hard to understand. It was all we could do to remind ourselves that God empathises with pain and suffering and that He is a loving God.

This was how we came to recognise what our own families must have been feeling, particularly our parents who would have had a double pain. Not only did they have the anguish over their grandchild to deal with but they were also hurting and worrying for us, their children.

As we were finally leaving the hospital, we spoke in the corridor with our oncology consultant who told us he was passing our case back to the dermatology department for future care. This was very significant as it indicated that they saw no need for oncology appointments for the time being - as if to say there was no active cancer around just now. No one could explain the mystery 'disappearance' of the cancer. It was doubtful whether the experimental alpha interferon had contributed much, but as the cause of the good news was unclear, no one wanted to disrupt a successful formula. A divergence of opinion emerged amongst the medics. We just thanked God, the real author of this reprieve.

I wasn't too concerned with the specific medical reason WHY Joshua was still alive - I was just so happy that he was. Tim, by contrast, was much more thorough in following the detail of the medical arguments and attempting to rationalise it all in order to make his own reasoned judgement. In his mind, the source of the medical controversy was the fact that Joshua was alive and well and for him that issue was clearly the direct result of God's intervention. Whilst he did not expect the medics to agree with his interpretation, he felt aggrieved that God's hand was not recognised. At an out patient appointment a while later, the oncologist asked us why we thought Joshua was still alive.

'It's down to God. You would not believe how many people are praying for Joshua,' I said, before Tim had a chance to open his mouth, surprising even myself.

'I see,' said Jon, as Tim reeled from the shock of my forth-rightness and we both wondered what Jon made of my bold and bald statement. Our inquisitiveness was soon answered as he dictated a progress report to our GP in which he expressed that he had 'not ruled out extra-terrestrial intervention' as the cause of Joshua's astounding good health!!

While others around us seemed to be rejoicing in Joshua's wellbeing as though he were cured, we still saw new lumps and found it hard to join them. A year of such disruption and varied emotions also brought a strain on our relationship, which was not always easy to deal with. We had to learn the hard way to accom-modate each other. We had clung tightly together in the crisis times but they had been so intense that we were left feeling drained of any emotional energy afterwards - even for months later. I felt as though I had used up all my reserves on Joshua and had nothing left to give my husband.

We were both handling it differently and, characteristic of our personalities, we were missing each other's cries for help. Inevitably, issues had arisen between us over the preceding year when our focus had rightly been on our valiant baby. It hadn't been the time to deal with them. During the 'easier' times that followed, communication on a deeper level needed to be restored and the backlog of unspoken problems resolved. It is always so much clearer in retrospect! At the time we were floundering. We looked to each other to heal our hurts but the hammering of the tough times was only just emerging. Neither of us could cope with each other's additional pain while we were in this state and we just kept digging up past issues, which remained unresolved. We seemed unable to stop bickering and Tim was feeling more alone than ever.

It culminated at a dinner party with two close friends when we tried to be funny but all our comments were coming out with barbed undertones of criticism towards each other. The row that followed was vitriolic! At this point we knew we had to do something about the brick walls and barriers we were presenting to each other. We had to bring in our mediators, John and Dawn, again. Their impartial listening was invaluable to us and by also praying with them, we were able to communicate again. It was never pleasant to share our relationship with another couple when we were fighting like this. We always felt bad with ourselves as we were made to face up to our wrong attitudes but we valued our marriage too much to bury things even further. We had reached an impasse, which required outside help and this support had been helpful to our relationship on a number of occasions.

We had also not been depending upon God in the same way during the easier times as we had been at the beginning. We still needed His help though and began to involve Him once more in the day to day aspects of our lives.

A key stepping stone came in the form of a Bible passage once more. Although it was the last thing I felt like doing just then, I had agreed to speak to a group of ladies, at Tim's mum's church, who had been praying for Joshua. I was also going to use the visit to take Joshua there to meet them all. As I was preparing what I was going to say, I just fell upon a paragraph in the Bible which leapt off the page at me and I knew it was another wonderful word from the Lord Himself. It reads,

> *We do not want you to be uninformed brothers about the hardships we suffered...We were under great pressure, far beyond our ability to endure, so that we despaired even of life. Indeed, in our hearts we felt the sentence of death. But this happened that we might not rely on ourselves but on God, who raises the dead. He has delivered us from such a deadly peril and He will deliver us. On Him we have set our hope that He will continue to deliver us, as you help us by your prayers. Then many will give thanks on our behalf for the gracious favour granted us in answer to the prayers of many.* [21]

These words were life itself to both of us. We were reassured that it was as though the Lord himself was telling us it was OK if we felt in despair and that He would help us. It was so exciting

---

[21] *2 Corinthians 1 v 8 - 11*

that we found ourselves reading it over and over, just knowing how it fitted our situation. So many people had already helped us by their prayers and when we thought back to the number of times God had answered in response, we were confident that 'many would indeed give thanks on our behalf'. So instead of wallowing in feeling low and alone, God had shown us that there was both purpose - in learning not to rely on ourselves but on God - and a positive outcome, whereby people would give thanks for the 'gracious favour granted us'. Of course this also tied up beautifully with the earlier important scripture for us in John 9, which had already convinced us that Joshua's life would bring glory to God. We still used that verse in John 9 in our praying for Joshua regularly. It was our lifeline if we ever doubted the sense of all we were going through.

Shortly afterwards, Tim was speaking to a church in Colchester, Essex about our experiences when Joshua demonstrated his outgoing personality once more by competing with his dad for the audience's attention. He did not need the microphone to out-shout daddy whenever Tim tried to say something! His extrovert nature was certainly established and made us all laugh and feel good again.

While we were at that church, we were also encouraged by a comment from one of many in the congregation whom Joshua had willingly reached out to for a cuddle; 'I have read about miracles and I have prayed for miracles, but today I have held a miracle.'

Our Joshua was growing up. He finally took his first steps outside his babywalker in May 1994, when he was sixteen months. Out of the blue one evening, he surprised himself and us by launching into the middle of the lounge from the sofa –

run, run, wobble splat! The wide eyes and mouth displayed his sheer delight at this new adventure and he was not at all put off by nose-diving the carpet...or the furniture, skirting boards, or even the kitchen tiles. Within a week he had gained himself a stitch in the forehead after a collision with a doorframe, but that was more traumatic for mummy than it was for him. We lived with our hearts in our mouths for a while as he began running everywhere long before he could slow down enough to walk. He learnt to hold his hands up high in the air ready to brace himself for the inevitable 'splat'. Although technique left a little to be desired, there was no faulting his determination. After a while of this, we learnt to accept his tumbles as well as he did but it was always funny taking him to other people's houses as no one could believe this manic little person who ran so fast but could not stop without falling on his face! It was several months before he slowed to a controlled trot and even then the hands were always up in the air ready for the impending fall! He was not daunted.

To keep him cool and looking more presentable, I took to shaving his hairy birthmarks at bath time and, with a bit of playful encouragement, he took to accepting his 'bzz bzz' as normal routine. Meanwhile, the hair on his head had now been cut to reveal an amazing mixture of golden blond with patches of darkest brown where some of the moles were on his head. The two-tone effect of colours was really striking and to us, yet another statement of his uniqueness. It was with a sense of pride that we began to appreciate there was nothing 'ordinary' about our boy.

People's names were Joshua's big learning point. Although his vocabulary grew slowly, the list of friends and family names he knew expanded rapidly. He was simply more interested in people than anything else. His favourite learning game would be

matching people to their families. Each time he learned a new
name, we would tell him the other members of that person's
family until he automatically started telling us. Then, as he saw
one person he would look and ask for the others. He was very
proud of himself for this social skill, but then we were proud of
him too. We would be driving in the car and occasionally he
would suddenly ask for someone whose name he remembered
and off we would go on the game of happy families again. By
now, Joshua's personality was so much bigger than his tiny frame.
At eighteen months he was weighing only twenty pounds and
stood just 75 cm tall but nobody could ignore him. After all, was
not everybody on this earth merely put there to entertain him?!

After stopping the interferon injections exactly a year after
they began, Joshua seemed to have a little growth spurt and his
appetite was improving slightly. However, at the same time,
there was also new growth in little lumps on the back of his head.
Immediately after another surgery in June, we were alarmed to
learn from our surgeon that he thought he had found some more
melanoma again, but when the results came through, they were
inconclusive. Once more, Joshua's life seemed on a knife-edge.

At home, I was more than busy trying to keep our bandage-
swathed child clean from food and vomit. It was a hot summer
and baths were out of the question, so it was a full-time occupa-
tion just rescuing his hair from his sticky fingers and picking him
up from even more tumbles than usual. He seemed oblivious to
the fact that his bandaged torso and arm and a lengthy operation
should have slowed him down. In reality, each operation did have
the effect of putting his walking and talking development a little
behind. He became less steady on his already wobbly feet for a
while and this of course frustrated him but did not diminish his

determination. I had to follow every wobbly trot, pacify every frustration and encourage him every waking hour. It was again an exhausting time of total uncertainty, a weird combination of anxiety and all-consuming child-care activity.

Because we could never escape the uncertainty over Joshua's future, we felt set apart from the families around us. No one could really empathise with us and although we knew many people loved us and faithfully prayed for us, there was still a feeling of isolation that only God could fill. One Sunday we listened to someone give an illustration about 'valley' experiences, which we believed to be very helpful. It is human nature to always want the 'mountain top' highs; no one wants to stay in a trough, so when we are there, we usually find ourselves moaning and fighting to get out. Then we miss the 'flowers' that are there in the valley - those beautiful little things that God provides for us along the valley floor which can only be appreciated if we actually notice them. Often, when we are feeling low, we see only the bad things and so we miss out, unless we make a point of looking at the blessings that are also there. We both found ourselves applying this picture to our lives and very soon realised that there were many 'flowers' there for us to appreciate, but they had to be spotted and even 'picked up'.

One of those 'flowers' was a local children's charity deciding to send us to Disney World in Florida, although before we went there were two more operations to face. On arrival in Florida we experienced our first tropical storm but it did nothing to dampen our spirits as there was so much to explore and enjoy. Only the stares and disguised whispers of other guests caught us off guard from time to time. At twenty-two months, we were all too aware that Joshua would soon be understanding what people

were saying about his appearance, so for his sake we found ourselves butting into others' conversations to explain. We accepted that it was the price we had to pay for such a privileged family
excursion.

It was a welcome respite before what was to come. Our 'valley' was about to deepen.

Chapter Seven:
To know God in His sufferings!

Tim Recounts

The first two months of 1995 found Coral and me chasing the hospital for a date to replace the operation cancelled in December. Although it had been originally scheduled as cosmetic, a residual lump on his neck from the previous operation in October had started to grow again. At the same time, another lump and yet another on the side of Joshua's neck were beginning to grow and bleed and we were both very concerned to get them dealt with.

Finally, along came operation number seventeen and with this New Year we met a new surgeon too. We were pleased that he concurred with our views of pressing ahead with cosmetic and preventative surgery. With higher trepidation than usual, I left Coral on the ward and carried Joshua into the anaesthesia room, all the time cradling him until he was unconscious from the 'smelly gas'. The theatre staff never did comment on my singing, as I sought to reassure Joshua with songs he would recognise.

Transferring to a new surgeon always made us feel a little vulnerable until we got to know him and his handiwork. It would have been much better for Joshua to have retained the same one throughout, not just for his sake, but for ours as well. Even so, we and many others frequently prayed for those operating on Joshua and we were rewarded with some of the best surgeons in the field of paediatric medicine.

We waited the usual couple of hours, then Joshua was returned from the operation with fresh wounds all over his face, hand and arm as well as two of the growing lumps in his neck having been cut out. However, the residual lump on the side of his neck was not touched, mainly because of its deeper position. It would have meant a tricky piece of surgery all by itself so the decision was taken just to watch it for the time being. We were both disappointed and relieved at the same time. Disappointed, for we knew any lump left behind would just continue to grow, but relieved that this surgeon was wise enough to stop in the face of undue risk to Joshua's life or of paralysis from severing a major artery or nerve. Coral was particularly pleased because there was such a dramatic difference to his face this time. Some moles had been completely removed and others reduced in size, although of course this first meant a lot of bruising and angry looking scars to begin with. We were used to seeing beyond them now.

More worrying was the news a week later that one of the lumps removed had been malignant. This time, the pathology report was categoric - the first definitely 'frank' malignancy for over a year, but there was worse to come.

On 20th March when I went to the hospital straight from work to collect the written results, the surgeon was extremely concerned. All he had seen when he opened Joshua's neck was a mass of black diseased lymph nodes - far too extensive to be cut out. The pathology report in his hands confirmed metastatic malignant melanoma - a major, serious development because it was the first time the cancer had been found outside Joshua's skin tissue. The surgeon was so concerned that I should see Joshua's primary doctor straight away that he frog-marched me down into the Outpatients' clinic and gatecrashed his appointments. Alarm bells were ringing loud and clear.

'Joshua needs to have all his neck lymph glands removed, but frankly this operation has never been done on a child. You won't get a paediatric surgeon to do the job. I have always been perfectly honest with you and there is so much we just don't know here. I'm afraid we need to check for secondary cancers again.'

The two days' exploratory tests became a week as, true to form, Joshua refused to be sedated with anything less than a general anaesthetic. We had experienced similar problems when he was younger but nothing was so traumatic for us all as the bone scan on this occasion. Having already had a light anaesthetic in the morning for a minor surgical procedure, Joshua refused to be sedated later that afternoon. The whole of his skeleton needed to be photographed to check for bone cancer secondaries. It required a series of seven or eight photographs and for each one Joshua needed to be stock still for five minutes at a time while the image formed on the monitor. After increasing the sedatives higher and higher and waiting hour after hour we tried in vain to persuade the doctors that this child could not be settled without total loss of conciousness. Eventually, it was decided to go ahead and hope he would stay still enough anyway. It must have been Joshua's biggest nightmare as five people struggled to hold him down for the series of pictures. The whole process took an agonising hour. Fighting the sedation and us the whole time, Joshua was hysterical. Coral was almost the same way by the end of this torture and I had to promise her we would NEVER allow such a traumatic process again. The sedatives only served to make him a liability as he struggled to run about in his 'normal' fashion, only to find that his legs were no longer doing what they should. He got angrier and angrier but did not give in. Worst for Joshua was the fact that we used restraint as a form of punishment when he had been naughty. We had quickly learnt that his pain threshold was so high that a smack on the hand made him laugh and was not effective for discipline. The poor boy felt severely punished to have five adults hold him down for an hour. Once more we found ourselves at new levels of exhaustion and perplexity. What did the future hold for our family?

I took the opportunity one evening to attend a conference at Wembley Arena where the speaker was Yonghi Cho, the Korean pastor with a church of some 700,000 people. He spoke from the Bible where Moses' hands were held up in prayer and Joshua won the battle.[22] It was true that by praying more, we were able to tap into God's peace in what could otherwise have become an intolerable wait. As we prayed, I was reminded of God's sovereignty in a fresh way. We would not give up on pushing the hospital for action, but whatever they did or did not do, ultimately God was in control. In the end it was God who gave us patience when medical help seemed too slow. Standing back from it all, our life was intolerably crazy. We had lived not for a few weeks or months facing dubious life expectancy, but for two years. As our love for and knowledge of Joshua grew and grew, so did the immense vulnerability and pain at the thought that he might die. Our son's very life had the fragility of a spider's web in the face of the marauding onslaught of cancer's cavalry and we were expending vast amounts of energy to stir the hospital into action. For the last eighteen months we had lived knowing that the doc-

---

[22] *Exodus 17 v 8 - 16*

tors we respected so much were on uncharted territory with no solutions or precedents to latch on to. Who would have thought three years before that two yuppie lifestyles would have come to this? And yet there was a tranquillity around us. We were drained, hassled and fatigued both physically and emotionally, far beyond our known capacity, but it felt like we were in the eye of the storm. It was a puzzle, an enigma unless you gave credit to two invisible aspects: prayer and God. In praying, the very core of our priorities was challenged: to see beyond our son's condition to God and to surrender to His purposes. But it was more than that. In surrender, just sensing Jesus with me and His willingness to help, reminded me that ultimately all is well. He has conquered even our worst enemy - death and that certainty of intimacy with Him through eternity brings hope for any situation.

The second aspect was the very presence of God Himself in our lives. Living a life that confronts life and death in the face daily causes you to refocus on what is really important. Ultimately God is the only certainty in life and eternity and despite the adversity, knowing and experiencing God personally was making us rich. We were regularly seeing unexplained changes in the way we felt, in restored strength and stamina and in hearing God speak clearly about which direction to take.

In short, our relationship with God had assumed a new dimension - we had been jolted out of mediocrity into new levels of interaction and relationship. In recognising that there is no greater thing than knowing Jesus, we were able to live in the eye of our storm and whilst aware of the whirlwind around us, be unruffled by it so long as we stayed trusting in Him. Isaiah puts it this way:

*You will keep him in perfect peace him whose mind is steadfast
because he trusts in you.*[23]

We needed to turn to God even more than before. Coral and
I could never really embrace the 'name it and claim it' style of
praying, for that seemed to be outside of the lessons God was
teaching us that 'what HE says happens'. Our approach was to
pray for Joshua's healing and also to ask God what His intentions
were so we could realign ourselves with His will. All He had told
us specifically so far was that His glory should be revealed
through Joshua, although we did not know how.

As Joshua's dad, I felt the weight of responsibility for my son
and for ensuring correct decisions for his treatment were taken
and carried out. The only thing that held me together was making myself worship God and listening to Christian tapes really
helped with that. The Lord did not answer our question of why
this was happening all over again, so I changed the question to,
'How do you want me to respond Lord?'

The answer came through the words of another song we sing
at church:

*We want to see Jesus lifted high...that all men may see the truth
and know, He is the way to Heaven.*[24]

So often the 'why?' question can mask a failure to deal with
the reality of something, can be a cover for self pity, or can be a
veiled fight against what has happened. In getting absorbed in it,
I could lose sight of what I knew: that Jesus deserves first place

---

[23] *Isaiah 26 v 3* [24] *We Want To See Jesus Lifted High, Doug Horley., Copyright © 1993
Kingsway"s Thankyou Music , PO Box 75, Eastbourne, East Sussex, BN23 6NW, UK. Used by
permission.*

in every circumstance and that He is the only way to knowing God the Father; that through His death and resurrection, eternal life is available to all who believe in Him and have a meaningful relationship now. The challenge for me was one of deeper acceptance that Joshua's condition had happened, that not even this tragedy could distort God's eternal perspective, nor the truth of the gospel. If others found God through Joshua's little life for example, then he would have achieved something of eternal value and purpose. Jesus would indeed be 'lifted high'.

Our experiences and circumstances were mere shadows of the suffering Jesus went through and with our right response, could help us 'to know You [Jesus] in Your sufferings'[25] as Graham Kendrick's song phrased it so eloquently.

I knew that we should confidently praise God, even in this circumstance. The fact that our son had survived this long with cancer growing so actively said to me that God's hand was on him. Part of the battle we were facing was to thank God for Joshua and to praise Him continually no matter what was going on. This was the only way we could get our focus of attention right again. There were moments when the enormity of Joshua's predicament hit me and it was in those moments that I recognised just how much strength, courage and stamina God was giving me the rest of the time! We had plenty to thank God for.

Back at home came the start of a series of difficult decisions. Although his ongoing good health had caused the doctors to question it several months before, Joshua's diagnosis was now beyond doubt - malignant melanoma. More than that, the pathology slides showed the disease to be very active and 'angry'.

---

[25] *Knowing You, - Graham Kendrick. Copyright © 1993 Make Way Music, PO Box 263, Croydon, Surrey CR9 5AP. Used by permission*

There was no explanation as to why Joshua was still alive, particularly as the pathology was identical to the biopsies taken in the first months of his life. It was almost as though Joshua's own immune system had been more than superhuman and had restricted the disease from spreading. Certainly, the country's leading expert in melanoma in Scotland was surprised to see more slides from our son, having expected him to have died a long time ago in infancy. She confirmed the melanoma diagnosis once more.

We were given three options for the coming months: to do nothing and let the disease take its natural course; to introduce chemotherapy (but that had not worked in the early months); or to re-introduce alpha interferon.

As always, the decision was very much a joint one between us and the doctors. They made it clear that they would be happy if we felt Joshua had had enough treatment altogether and we wanted to stop at any stage. It would not have surprised them if we wanted to give up and we almost felt that they would prefer us to do so.

Still, we settled on restarting interferon, particularly because our past experience showed Joshua should suffer no ill effect. It came as something of a surprise then when he did get into difficulties. We expected the drug to give him a fever and general malaise for the first week or two, but unfortunately, after the first week, Joshua's liver objected and a form of hepatitis was diagnosed. After a month of struggling with it, interferon was sadly abandoned. We were still praying for the purity of his blood. However, by the end of June we were all very worried by the dramatic increase in the size of these new neck tumours. One had doubled over two weeks and a new deeper growth was now visible. Various meetings were held at Great Ormond Street and at one time it was muted that the lumps were inoperable.

Finally we were introduced to Professor Spitz who, according to the *Daily Telegraph*,[26] is still reputed to be the top paediatric surgeon in Britain. He agreed to perform surgery on Joshua. At least, he agreed to debulk the mass but his availability to do so meant a further wait of at least a month and total removal of such a large and complicated tumour would not be possible. This additional delay was intolerable but nothing could be done to create an earlier appointment. Naturally, while we waited, a bigger tumour would also mean a bigger scar but, in this, we were as little concerned as the doctors about cosmetic appearance. By now, the scarring on Joshua's neck was so bad that any more would make very little difference. Coral dressed him permanently in high collars or polo necks anyway and more scars were as nothing compared to the appearance of these purple and bleeding cancerous protrusions.

Finally, we reached the date to go into hospital for Joshua's neck surgery: July 21st 1995. As far as we were concerned, it was not before time. The tumour was now growing so rapidly that we saw visible change over each 24-hour period. It was distending his neck out behind his ear and even his face was becoming distorted by the multiple lumps that had emerged. On the day before, we were warned that the operation was major and a bed in Intensive Care had been booked in anticipation of his losing large amounts of blood. We were told he would certainly need morphine after theatre and would lose the ability to shrug his left shoulder. He could also sustain some damage to facial

---

[26] *17 May 1988*

nerves, so it was not without stress that Joshua was offered up for his 20th operation. Many people were praying hard that day.

For his most serious surgery so far, thankfully, Joshua was first on the morning theatre list. From what could be seen on the surface, there were tumours growing on top of tumours. We were warned that it was impossible to know just how deep this mass went, or what it had entangled itself with, until the professor opened up Joshua's neck. We were under no false hopes. The surgeon made the risks very clear to us. Yet, we were prayerfully optimistic of success. It was scary, but seeing God answer our prayers so regularly gave us confidence to get through the day. Within minutes of returning from surgery, Joshua had already pulled out one drip from his vein. Only a couple of hours later, he was running around the corridors like an escaped prisoner. Professor Spitz could hardly believe his eyes.

'This child ought to be in intensive care,' he said on his evening ward round, as Joshua ran up to him and hit him over the head with a helium balloon. 'I cannot believe how well he looks after such a major operation. If it were you or I, we would be in agony and laid up recovering.'

We just smiled, as this was very usual for our son post-operatively and we were very used to handling the positive delight and surprise of surgeons. Clearly, prayer works, repeatedly. The operation was considered a big success, although there was a huge indentation to Joshua's neck where the diseased glands had been and, as expected, some rather massive scars. Even we were surprised to learn that the largest lump had reached the size of a satsuma.

A few days after the surgery we all escaped to the coast for a holiday. With Joshua's love of sand and thriving development, the hideousness of the growing disease could almost be forgotten. By God's grace, we were enjoying our son and, outside the hospital, he was loving life more than anyone we knew. Joshua was living in blissful ignorance of his condition even though by now he would occasionally point to his birthmarks and seemed aware that they were there.

On the outside everything seemed to be going so well, yet there was a stark contrast between the apparent health and vitality our son was displaying and the relentless progression of the tumours. The beauty of his developing character seemed to contradict the ugliness of the cancer and we lived with this paradox. Our next visit to GOS at the end of August turned into a rather grim consultation with Doctor Harper, our consultant dermatologist there. The pathology reports from the big operation the previous month revealed a significant deterioration in Joshua's condition. It was beyond all doubt that the lymph nodes removed by Professor Spitz contained metastatic disease, which meant that it was spreading or invading tissue other than the original site. Joshua's plight was described as very serious indeed and we were advised that if we wished to continue treatment, we would need to take a more drastic course of action. There was even evidence already of a new lump in Joshua's neck.

Once again the black cloud of harsh experimental chemotherapy was looming over us and we would have to make difficult decisions. Once more the various consultants needed to pool their wisdom and draw up yet more experimental options to present to us. I could understand why Coral was tempted to delude herself as she found it too painful to believe God would let him die. After all, for her, the hard work of rearing a sick baby was finally giving way to enjoying a happy child. For me, the problems only seemed to be intensifying. Joshua had reached an age when we needed to get him onto a waiting list for Nursery and Primary school. That was weird. We were not used to long-term thinking and planning any more. We were dutifully shown around our chosen school and listened to the head teacher. All looked great - except would he be alive by the age of four to start attending? Yet he was so very much full of life and energy - a real bundle of fun and cheekiness - that on most days we could not imagine life without him. While other toddlers stuck close to their parents on the school tour, Joshua was off introducing himself to the bemused children in the classrooms and 'helping' them with their work! We seemed to live on two levels. We had to plan for his future without even knowing if he had one. That was normality for us and utter abnormality for most others around us.

The decision-making only got harder with time. Our only option was to give up on medicine or make him very ill in an attempt to save his life, with no guarantees it would work. The sense of isolation caused by these circumstances really hurt. Who could relate to our pain? Who had experienced such difficult times and who could advise us? Our friends and families were very supportive but there remained a level of pain that seemed beyond the reach of them all.

Finally, God Himself began to ease the burden, as indeed He always promises to do. It was through praying with a friend that I gained fresh recognition and understanding of what Jesus must have suffered. This brought me comfort and relief and reduced the sense of isolation that our circumstances made me feel.

We would never have chosen such suffering for Joshua and yet Christ chose even greater pain to bring salvation to us. As I struggled with the idea once more that Joshua might die, I was again astounded that God the Father actually CHOSE to give His Son Jesus to die so that mankind might have life. While this very thing is central to the gospel, the emotional content is unfathomable. It only begins to make sense when we recognise God's love for us as the hymn *How Great Thou art*[27] expresses it:

> *And when I think that God His Son not sparing,*
> *Sent Him to die, I scarce can take it in.*
> *That on the cross my burden gladly bearing*
> *He bled and died to take away my sin*

A verse in the Old Testament book of Habakkuk was also helpful at this point:

> *though the fig tree does not bud and there are no grapes on the vines…yet will I rejoice in the Lord, I will be joyful in God my saviour.*[28]

The whole verse speaks about the prophet's ability to 'rejoice and be joyful in God' even when natural expectations were thwarted and not happening. How true this was for us! In nature, blossom and fruit are the normal cycle, which rarely fails. So too, one does not expect children to die. The natural cycle is that they outlive you. When that cycle is threatened with disruption, despair, depression and immense pain loom, as the prophet experiences earlier in the book of Habakkuk. What had changed in him in the intervening verses? His focus of attention. He switched from only seeing the awfulness of the national plight

---

[27] *O Lord My God, How Great Thou Art, Stuart K Hine (1899-1989). Copyright © 1953 Stuart K Hine/Kingsway's Thankyou Music, PO Box 75, Eastbourne, East Sussex BN23 6NW, UK. Worldwide (Excluding USA & Canada). Used by permission.* [28] *Habakkuk 3 v 17, 18*

into seeing the God still in control behind the circumstance. I too needed constantly to make the same transition.

There was nothing good about the latest medical developments, but I was reminded that we do not have to be dependent upon things going right in our lives in order to praise God. God's love is constant through good and bad times and I found that giving thanks and praise during the broken times brought strength and healing from some of the pain.

How would we choose between the very stringent cocktail of 'chemo-immunotherapy' and palliative care - the technical term for just making someone as comfortable as possible before they die? The drug combination had never been given to a child before but, from the adult patients, we knew it would be very toxic. It would take Joshua to the brink of death to try to beat the disease once and for all. The body's organs would be pushed to their very limits and could even be in failure for a few days before switching back. But between these two extremes, all the anecdotal statistics indicated notably higher life expectancy in chemo-immuno patients than in those who just had one or the other. As the treatment would continue over several months, it would be our longest ever stint as in-patients, with the probability of Joshua needing to go into Intensive Care.

We were really at the cutting edge of innovative cancer treatment. The top consultants and professors from St Bartholomew's and also from the Royal Marsden Hospital (famous for its specialism in cancer treatment) had become involved in our case, not to mention further advice from Europe and the USA. Joshua was of such interest to the medical world. A few experiments under preparation with gene therapy were briefly investigated on our behalf, but as yet these were not sufficiently developed to risk on a child. There really was nothing else.   Chemo-immuno therapy was our last hope medically speaking, if we were willing to take the risk.

Beyond all of this, our focus was still on God's ability to heal, whether that be directly or through the drugs. We were constantly reminding ourselves to entrust Joshua to God, as only He has the power to give or take life. Deciding whether or not to go with the drugs did not detract from this; we still had to trust God and we still had to face the very real possibility of losing our son. Perhaps our decision was brave, perhaps it was out of desperation, I'm not really sure, but all the time we were conscious of our need for God.

When we tried to project how we would feel if Joshua died and we hadn't tried this last treatment, we were both certain that we would have regrets. Also, on hearing how bad the side-effects were, we were partly torn apart, but partly reassured that through prayer we had always seen our boy sail through better than expected. It was a real challenge in this decision to sift our thoughts so we could be clear that we were facing the dangers honestly. We were trying to discern whether it was God's will to put him through this, or whether we were just over-confident after past successes and thus diminishing the risk in our minds. In the end we felt a quiet confidence that it was the right thing and this was backed up later by our church leadership's independent discernment. Joshua's life was all too precious to us.

So it was after many meetings, telephone conversations, discussions with our church leaders, prayers and heart searching that we decided to go on with more treatment. We reasoned that our little fighter son had not given up, so neither could we. He was so incredibly brave that he probably would have chosen it for himself if he were old enough to understand.

At the same time as all this turmoil, it was a welcome distraction that our new baby was about to be born.

Chapter Eight:

And Misha makes two...

Coral Recounts

I was delighted when I found myself pregnant again. We had always wanted more than one, but up until then we had been kept too busy with the medical needs of our first baby to entertain the idea of another. I was somewhat anxious about how I would cope though, with Joshua already being such a demanding little person; but with much reassurance from people close to us, we had made up our minds. Then of course came the fears that many pregnant women face about the health of their unborn child. But in my case I could not entertain for one moment having a baby without something being wrong. Because it was my only experience so far, it was hard to imagine anything else. Even so, I reassured myself, surely it could never be as bad again as having a disfigured child who might not live. Statistically, we had been warned that for us there was a higher risk of having another child with complications and we also had more chance of the birthmarks occurring again. Even so, we wanted a sibling for our son so it was a risk worth taking. All these things went over and over in my mind, but whatever happened I wanted this baby.

A week in hospital suspecting an ectopic pregnancy was not a good start. Then there were frequent scans and measurements. One time I was even told that the baby seemed out of proportion and some of Joshua's medication may have put the foetus at risk, so we were constantly praying for its wellbeing. No test existed to detect possible defects of the skin so we would have to wait it out.

I was not too pleased with the idea of a Halloween baby but when my labour started on the night of 30th October I was more than ready for the big event. Contractions were persistent through the night so we phoned my friend Ruth to babysit Joshua and drove up to the labour ward at six the next morning. Upon arrival, everything seemed to slow down but Joshua was scheduled for two days of pre-treatment tests the very next day and Tim could not risk having to choose which hospital to be in. We had little choice but to give in to the doctor's intervention to hurry things along. It was a wonderful birth. The labour ward knew us already through Joshua and treated us like royalty. We had the personal service of the consultant throughout and a wonderful midwife who stayed beyond her shift to see it through. Their attentiveness to us was exemplary. When they told me that the baby was lying on my spine, it did not take much to talk me into an epidural. Suddenly, the contractions hurt no more and it was pure joy from then on.

Misha Jemma Jade was born just after 3 p.m. into a room charged with emotion. I was fully alert, out of pain and even able to determine exactly when to push the baby out. The tears flowed freely as our perfect little doll emerged without a birthmark in sight. Even the medical staff were crying and we were all so busy looking for blotchy skin that it was a full ten minutes before anyone bothered to confirm the sex of our baby! Surprisingly, she had dark hair and at 6lb 5oz, she was even smaller than Joshua at birth; but Misha was clearly healthy and our relief and thankfulness to God were intense.

As Misha was born there came to us that ecstatic feeling which parents talk about at the birth of their first child but which we had never experienced. Tears of joy were finally ours and just for a brief while, we could focus on our perfect baby. She had beautiful big blue eyes, set in a round face. She was just perfect in every sense. Above all, we had a healthy baby. Whatever had caused the genetic mis-copy with Joshua had not been repeated. I could hardly wait to show her to Joshua.

'Baby sister, baby sister!' I could hear him shouting as he ran down the corridors, even before I could see him. He brought a smile to my face and thankfully to most of the other new mums resting on their beds. It was a special moment and we captured it on videotape, as Joshua met Misha for the first time. He had been well prepared and was often heard to say, 'Baby sleeping,' as he put his hand on my tummy, but as patience was not one of his strengths, it was never for long enough to feel a kick. His other frequent comment was, 'Baby out soon,' which told us that he was looking forward to meeting her. He knew he was going to have a baby sister and already he had managed to let out our secret to an inquisitive friend.

With his usual lack of concentration, after a brief meeting he was off to introduce himself to all the nurses. He felt particularly at home in any hospital and ran off looking for his bed. So, at the sight of him pulling back curtains on a weary but bemused mum, he was quickly taken off the premises and I was left to rest until Tim could return to bring me home two days later.

Visitors who arrived to meet Misha for the first time had to be closely vetted for their health. It was not for her sake but for Joshua, who could not catch so much as a cold to upset the timing of his next vital treatment or the operation, which would be needed first. We found ourselves screening everyone and it did reduce the number of visitors for our new baby quite considerably.

The joy of our new daughter was not totally unblemished as we were dreading the harsh effects of Joshua's imminent new treatment. On top of that, all the practical difficulties of living in hospital with Joshua and coping with our new baby were somewhat daunting. Although we tried to enjoy this special couple of weeks getting to know Misha, the unstoppable growth on Joshua's face and neck was a constant reminder of the awfulness yet to come. It was not so much the delight brought by our new baby that helped us through this time, as God's word. How incredible that a book written so long ago could be so relevant and helpful, yet the Bible seemed to really sum up for us how we felt and help us to be more determined in pursuing God to supply all we were about to need. As the years were passing we were building up a treasure chest of special moments with God, even though we were feeling battered by our circumstances. The Apostle Paul describes his own experience as follows:

We are hard pressed on every side, but not crushed; perplexed but not in despair; persecuted but not abandoned; struck down, but not destroyed. We always carry around in our body the death of Jesus, so that the life of Jesus may also be revealed in our body.[29]

This is a central theme in Christianity, that in order to know Jesus, to be 'alive' to God, we have to 'die' to ourselves - we have to identify with the death and resurrection of Jesus. In practical terms this means switching our rules for His rules, learning to

---

[29] *2 Corinthians 4 v 8 - 10*

put God first in everything - above self, job, promotion, even partner and family.

Living a life in which we faced daily the potential mortality of our son caused a realignment of all our normal expectations, ambitions and desires. More than ever we realised just how real an experience knowing Jesus is and the assurance of eternity. Everything we face in life, bad or good, is but a shadow when compared with Jesus's own suffering and God's gift to us of everlasting life. But God's gift to us is also 'here and now'.

God promises to give us (and our experiences prove that He does) the life of Jesus within us - a strength to endure more than we thought possible; to know peace in the midst of the storm, hope in the face of hopelessness and ultimately, in the words of Kendrick's song, 'so with You (Jesus) to live and never die'...

Not even the joy of a perfect new baby beats having a relationship with God. It's the ultimate deal.

Chapter Nine:

Not without hope

Coral Recounts

As we moved our newly expanded family into GOS once more, I was dreading the prospect of keeping Joshua entertained while he was attached by a Hickman Line to a drip stand. The requisite operation to insert his new line gave me comparatively little concern.

'Don't worry, he'll only be hooked up for an hour to start with,' the nurse reassured me. That was frightening enough. He had so much irrepressible energy that he was unable to stay in one room for five minutes, let alone in one corner for an hour. I was terrified that he would trip over and pull out the newly inserted Hickman Line. Misha was passed to any convenient visitor, parent or nurse as I chased Joshua continually and with more than a little anguish, I tried to train him to remember his drip - or at least to slow down. Obviously, he was unused to such restraint and was clearly frustrated. That first hour of being 'attached' confirmed my worst fears of how hard it would be. When we were told that, from the next day onwards, the drip would be a permanent part of him twenty-four hours a day for ten days, my worst nightmare was reinforced.

Then, to everyone's surprise and by some miracle, the second time his line was put into use, he just accepted the situation. We called the drip stand his 'Robby Robot' and he repeated our shouts of, 'Joshua, remember Robby Robot!' as we disentangled his feet and allowed him to explore the playroom and corridors on the ward. This bizarre contraption followed reluctantly behind. To my astonishment, it became a great game to push his great, heavy drip stand everywhere himself and my prayers were answered as he even responded to the pleas to slow down. I was so thrilled that he continued to enjoy himself that it made up for the difficulties, at least in part.

It was much harder work now with two children but Joshua showed only love for his baby sister and not a hint of jealousy. She became a useful distraction, like an additional toy for him to cuddle whenever he wanted, or to pose with for a photograph. Every time a new visitor arrived, Joshua would greet them, then point out his new sister.

'Cuddle Misha!' he would command, regardless of whether they were family, friend or medical staff. Then, 'Come here,' 'Light on,' 'Shut dee door,' 'Get phone,' 'See Joshla,' 'Milk peez,' 'Dink a water peez,'… He was in his element with so many people constantly running to his commands. We had to laugh at the wisdom of putting Joshua's room opposite the nurses' station because every time he saw someone return to the desk, they would be summoned into his room. It simply delighted him to see people do as he asked and he had a smile for everyone. Usually that was all they got - a big cheeky grin, but it was enough for most.

The end of an infusion on the drip would be indicated by an alarm sounding and the same noise would be heard if a child stood or sat on the line, preventing its flow. Needless to say, there were constant alarms coming from at least one of the ten cubicles on our ward and it seemed to be from Joshua's more than most. Every time it went off, he would be heard calling out, 'Oh beeping again, Nurses,' or even to our amazement and amusement, using the technical term 'Nurse! Come quick! Occluded again!' I started to wonder whether he was obstructing his line deliberately for the effect it had of bringing people to him. Either way, everyone soon knew Joshua had arrived on the ward!

Having completed the first course of chemo with no obvious ill effect whatsoever, it was time for immunotherapy. As far as anyone knew, Joshua was one of the youngest children ever to receive the most toxic of the immunotherapy drugs - Interleukin.

At first nothing happened, then he began to lose his appetite. By the third day, the effects very quickly accelerated. Our borderline hyperactive toddler suddenly took to his bed. His skin, particularly on his limbs, became purple/red sore, hot and swollen and his temperature soared. He became uncharacteristically lifeless and refused to be touched. He had lost all his energy and yet he couldn't sleep properly. Although we thought we were prepared, the sudden deterioration was devastating and made worse as the symptoms increased. He looked like a poor little purple 'Michelin' man. Our anxiety peaked when he did not make a quick recovery at the end of the five-day course as predicted. Just when he should have been feeling better from the immunotherapy, the effects of the chemotherapy kicked in. The delayed reaction was quite normal and we were assured that the adult patients on this drug combination suffered the same uncomfortable effects and worse, but still it came as a shock to see Joshua this unwell. We had been praying for God to protect him from such harsh side-effects and I was particularly upset that these prayers did not seem to be being answered. Then his blood counts started to fall and any prospect of taking him home for a few days break quickly evaporated.

'It really is quite normal,' the experts tried to comfort us. 'You should remember we were preparing for intensive care but he's holding his own. All the vital signs are good.'

As the long days passed slowly, his high temperature caused concern even with the doctors. No one knew if it was just a side-effect of the Interleukin or if Joshua's Hickman Line was once again infected.

I was back to living one day at a time. Misha, like most one-month-old babies had me up several times in the night for feeding. My anguish over Joshua was profound and in this, Tim and I shared the pain of seeing him go through so much. Even the medical staff, as well as the other parents on our ward, were impacted by the sudden change in character. It was similar to the early days when Joshua was first born and lack of sleep (this time through Misha) compounded my anxiety. We realised what a tremendous gift those intervening brief months of having Joshua free from obvious cancer had been, as this renewed threat to his mortality was causing such a deep pain in both of us. Yet again, God was there with an encouragement. Through a blurry haze of exhaustion, we felt the following words reassured us not to back out, however hard it seemed;

And the God of all grace, who called you to his eternal glory in Christ, after you have suffered a little while, will Himself restore you and make you strong, firm and steadfast. [30]

We just had to go through this time. As we and others prayed, there was no sense that we were wrong with the original deci-

---
[30] *1 Peter 5 v 10*

sion to go with the treatment. So here in the Bible was a promise of restoration following our period of suffering. Looking back now, we know that to be true.

Living with other sick children and parents brought an intuitive understanding and bond and we forged good friendships as we shared each other's joys when our children got good results or did well and genuine sadness when the opposite occurred. Also, we soon recognised the frayed nerves, which manifested as flippancy, anger, frustration or withdrawal in all of us at some time and this brought a sense of 'safety between sufferers'. Deep pain is so intimate to the person experiencing it that even if they are well meant, trite platitudes can come across as clumsy intrusions into the fragility of one's soul.

Joshua enjoyed being with the other children. He enjoyed learning their names, the names of their parents and other siblings and doing his usual 'happy families' game. If he did not see one of them on a given day, he would ask after them.

'Where Jamie gone? Where Sam? Where Scott?'

When told that they weren't very well that day, he would say, 'Oh get dee doctor. Get Pitchard!' nodding assuredly at his wise pronouncement, displaying implicit trust in the doctor's skill to make all things better.

There were many special friends among the patients on the ward but perhaps the most loved by Joshua was ten-year-old Jamie Gritton, who was in for his second long stay of treatment and Jamie liked to pay us little visits to see the new baby. He soon became a very helpful babysitter as Misha often wanted a cuddle at awkward moments. I was grateful to have someone to pass her to.

I now appreciated the timing of Misha's arrival, having been frustrated by not conceiving our second child as soon as we hoped. It turned out to be God's perfect timing for us. Had she been even a few months older, this life in hospital would have been so much harder. The intensity of our situation with Joshua was lessened by having Misha to enjoy as well. As we watched other patients on the ward with school-age siblings having to divide their time between hospital and home, we counted ourselves very fortunate. Misha was a pure delight and blessing and would never remember this traumatic time.

Joshua completed the first course of his treatment and went straight onto the second just before Christmas (1995). Our best ever Christmas present came in the form of visible shrinkage in the once enormous tumours along his left jaw line. The four or five round swellings, each an inch or so across, became soft first, then noticeably began to reduce in size. For the first few days we did not dare believe our eyes, but when the doctors also noticed, we allowed our excitement to take root. It was the first time Joshua's cancer had ever responded to drugs and this gave us a sense of hope, which helped us through the pain of seeing him so unwell. Such a positive result helped the medics to decide on continuing the treatment without a break. They even began to talk about a potential third course, but this came with the warning that unless we saw 90% shrinkage by the end of the second course, such aggressive action would not be continued. There was real concern that Joshua's vital organs would not survive such toxic hammering indefinitely. Either way, it would mean spending Christmas, New Year and his birthday in hospital. That was the least of our worries though. Christmas on the ward would be very different but I was quite sure we could make it a special day. Although Tim could never fully escape the gravity of

Joshua's predicament in the same way, the combination of Joshua's excitement and shrinking tumours was enough to make me quite high that Christmas Day. There were so many presents that opening them became a daily event until January 8th, including his birthday too.

A pattern had emerged with the treatment which saw Joshua generally spending a week in bed completely debilitated, a week slowly recovering, then more drugs to knock him down again. According to the day in the drug regime schedule, we could roughly predict how he would be. He ought to have been well for his birthday.

But Joshua's third birthday was not a good day. Throughout our stay, he had been having trouble keeping his temperature down, until finally an infection in his blood was confirmed and it was not responding to the antibiotics. This meant he had to have an emergency operation to remove the infected Hickman Line, or the infection could back up into his heart. I was so disappointed for him; I even had a cake and party organised. He had been refusing food and drink for some weeks but was just deciding he wanted to eat again, when we had to deny him food for the general anaesthetic.

It must have been quite obvious how stressed I had become, because the following day it was suggested that we take the children home for a break. Another operation to reinsert a Hickman Line would not happen until after the weekend anyway. So we took advantage of this opportunity - the first in six weeks. Joshua's delight at his own bedroom and all his own toys again was very rewarding, but his muscle wastage and general weakness made him a shadow of his former self and energies. When we returned to our cubicle on Robin Ward two days later, I watched proudly as our excited Joshua breezed onto the ward calling, 'Hi, I'm back, Joshla here. Hi nurses!' His expectation of a grand welcome was met as staff and fellow patients responded to his cheeky cheerfulness. We were feeling refreshed from our first weekend at home so Tim went back to work as usual. Inserting a line was such a minor operation he did not even stay around for it. Imagine our disappointment after all we had been through to rid Joshua of his original line infection, to learn that it was back again in his new line a few days later.

On 22nd January 1996 we watched a television documentary about the development of a radical melanoma vaccine in Los Angeles. We were fascinated to learn more about Doctor Morton and his experiment there in the USA. It was an exciting treatment, which had been trialling for some ten to fifteen years. It worked in the same way as traditional vaccines, by stimulating the body's immune system to produce certain antibodies to attack cells injected into the patient.

It made a lot of sense for Joshua's unique case, because being born with the cancer, the biggest hurdle seemed to be to get his body to recognise it as something foreign. Moreover, his immune system had already proved its own natural strength in keeping the cancer from spreading to any vital organ for the last three years. Joshua's tumours seemed to be reducing nicely with the chemo-immunotherapy; however, they were still reasonably large. We did not know if they would ever be sufficiently reduced to make the vaccine a viable option for us. The patients who seemed to have success with this American treatment were the fortunate ones who could first have most, if not all, of the cancer surgically removed. As we watched the television programme we wondered whether it might be an option one day and determined to ask our doctors more about it. We certainly did not realise just how soon we would find out directly for ourselves.

On 25th January (this time Tim's birthday), I noticed a new growth in front of Joshua's ear and another tiny one at the back of his neck. This was later confirmed by the consultants and it meant extremely bad news. Even though the older tumours had shrunk by over 50% and Joshua was getting stronger despite the drugs, these new growths meant that some of the cancer had changed to become resistant to the treatment. Chemo-immunotherapy had failed.

We were devastated. Even more so when it was decided to abandon the third course of treatment. This was immensely painful for us. Tim in particular found the decision to stop treatment exceptionally hard to accept and wrote several letters to the consultants laying out his arguments for continuing. In the end the doctors were resolute.

Very abruptly, we were brought to the end of the curative era at Great Ormond Street and our pain was intense. Here was the finish of three years of valiant effort on all parts to beat the disease. Within the last month we had finally seen the results longed for as, at last, the tumours shrank before our eyes in response to drugs. We had seen surgical success when he was a baby, but had never seen a biological response until now. We were catapulted from our highest point to our lowest within a matter of days. What would we do now? We had felt 'safe' in the environment of the hospital where everything possible was being done to help Joshua beat this illness. Now, all too suddenly, it was over. We were being told that hope was gone, but we could not give up our hope.

When Professor Spitz was called in again to see Joshua, this eminent surgeon eventually agreed he could again attempt an operation on the remaining tumours and perhaps debulk them by some 80%. However, he would only be prepared to embark upon such risky and major work if it was considered medically worthwhile.

'After all, there's a limit to how many times you can chop into a child's neck if the thing keeps regrowing,' he reasoned quite frankly. He would only agree to operate if we would be following up his surgery with more effective treatment to stop it coming back. We had thoroughly exhausted all the medical options available to us in the UK but we were still not ready to give up. The professor himself was astounded at Joshua's resilience to the recurrent disease, not to mention the harsh treatments. But as long as our son was fighting so hard, how could we stop?

There was just one final remote possibility of a cure and it meant a trip to Los Angeles within the week. Time now was of the essence. We knew from past experience that the rate of regrowth would be dramatic.

When our doctors telephoned him, the American specialist was initially reluctant to take Joshua on but he agreed to see us at least before rejecting him outright. Typical of our personalities, we had mixed feelings when the first fax came through. Tim was cautious and anxious, seeing all the pitfalls and practicalities that needed attention. On the other hand he was also clear-headed and able to ensure nothing got missed. He was torn. He was not ready to give up on finding a cure for Joshua, but he had remained sceptical of the vaccine's chances. Even I had to admit that medical opinion about this treatment was diverse and the detractors of the vaccine attributed much to the radical skill of

Doctor Morton as one of the top surgeons in the States. The TV documentary also highlighted the social impact of monthly trips to the West Coast USA, and some patients had faced financial ruin, redundancy and family strain. I knew we would all have to go at first and Misha was still only three months old. Even so, if Doctor Morton would accept Joshua…

I was experiencing such a rush of adrenaline and, with nervous excitement, dashed about trying to do far too much all at the same time. For me, the new hope, however small, was very stimulating but the stress could have been overwhelming if it were not for the support we received from all around us. All our arrangements were made while we were still at the hospital and we still had to get home and unpack our life after three months there before we could pack again!

As our house had been burgled shortly after our visit home (and tragically we lost our camcorder and all the film of Joshua and Misha), there was a new camcorder to buy. Then there were phone calls to be made, tickets to collect, not to mention new shoes for Joshua and the normal things of feeding and caring for two such dependent young children - all happening at once. So it went on. At least we had both children already on our passports, thanks to an instinct some weeks ago that such an emergency trip might one day be necessary.

As if by way of confirmation that we were doing the right thing, a volunteer helper on the ward, Betina, who had become one of our many friends there, produced £2,500 for the trip. It so happened that she lived next door to the chairman of a London firm that gave regularly to charity and it was the encouragement we needed not to let the potential expense of it all deter us. As if we needed any more confirmation, we were then prom-

ised free plane tickets from the ward psychologist, whose close
friend just 'happened' to have a senior job in British Airways. As
far as I was concerned, the Lord definitely wanted us to make
this trip. I had never seen so much achieved so quickly.

Even so, I could not help adding my tears to Tim's as we said
goodbye to Robin Ward, the doctors, nurses, other parents and
friends. Joshua was feeling better and was jumping up and down
on his bed telling everyone that he was going to see 'Mickey
Mouse', but we wept. It was an emotional time, a watershed for
us. The hospital had been our second home through thick and
thin. For thirty-six months it had provided such excellent partnership in the determined search for a cure and from now on it
would leave that partnership. We felt jettisoned out of our warm
security blanket into the unknown. We knew that on our return
our relationship with the hospital would be on a completely different footing. We had little choice but to throw ourselves on
God's mercy.

Within just four hectic days of receiving Donald Morton's fax
and deciding to go, we were on a plane to California to meet the
man for ourselves.

Chapter Ten:
When God directs
Tim Recounts

J oshua was regaining strength daily and his lively, cheeky personality was re-emerging. As Coral, the children and I sat outside McDonalds in Heathrow's Terminal 4 building, waiting to board our flight, his excitement at going to see Mickey Mouse spilled out.

Once I had said a tentative 'yes - we will go' everything fell into place with remarkable ease and clarity. I was still dumbfounded that such good airline tickets had been donated to us, at short notice and at flight times that coincided with our appointment schedule. Although my misgivings about the trip were immense, evidences of God's provision flowed thick and fast. Once on board the twelve-hour flight and with both children asleep, my mind mulled over the extraordinary events of the previous few days.

Even though my staff were facing a critical time on our project at work, my managers had told me, 'Family comes first - just go.' Then there was the donation of money to cover the expenses of the first trip - accommodation, car hire, the medical bills. And all of this happened within the space of just a few days before we had even left the hospital! I was stunned, but it was only the beginning.

While I was thinking about all this, Coral got chatting with a lady who turned out to be the Australian co-ordinator for Revival Ministries International, Rodney Howard Brown's group of churches. Unusually, it was our tiny second child who first grabbed her attention and the reason they started their conversation. Her husband was also on the flight and they were so moved by our story that they asked if they could put us on their prayer networks in Australia. It had to be a divine meeting that caused Joshua now to be prayed for in four continents of the world. The very thought was both humbling and awe inspiring. Everywhere we went, God was directing us to His family. As soon as we arrived in our rented apartment in Santa Monica we met the teenage daughter in the apartment below us, who was also a Christian and offered to pray.

We met with Doctor Morton's associate on the first day, to hand over all the medical reports for their briefing. This was followed by our meeting with Doctor Morton himself on Valentine's Day, to hear his decision. It was so funny to see Joshua take control of the interview by grabbing both Doctor Ollila and Doctor Morton by the hand. He made them sit on the floor with him whilst he introduced himself with a cheerful,

'Hi, I'm Joshla, this Misha. Here Tim and Cowol!' with a little giggle as he clasped his hands as if to start doing business.

I feigned a 'Don't be so cheeky Joshua,' but the sight of these two eminent doctors obeying a three-year-old's demand to sit cross-legged on the floor was irresistibly amusing, as well as reassuring that they were connecting with him.

Still suffering from jetlag and somewhat bewildered, we were not sure whether to be pleased with the outcome. Almost immediately, Doctor Morton agreed he could only take Joshua onto the vaccine programme if the tumour could first be substantially reduced. When pressed, we learnt that his definition of substantial was about a 90% reduction and Professor Spitz had only pre-

dicted 80% at best. Even worse, the tumour was already growing again at speed and we found a new lump under his chin when
he stretched his head back that same day - it was already the size
of a gobstopper. I knew that it would be touch and go whether
Joshua would meet the acceptance criteria.

Whilst in the clinic that afternoon, another important meeting happened. Since our arrival in Santa Monica, I had been trying unsuccessfully to reach another pastor friend in nearby Santa
Barbara, as he had promised to put me in touch with a church in
Santa Monica. It was now Thursday and I was frustrated that we
had not made contact. I noticed whilst we were waiting for
Doctor Morton that one of the ladies who worked there was
wearing a chain with a dove on it. Pat Mullen seemed to be a
really efficient, friendly lady, so I quizzed her about the dove on
her necklace. Sure enough, Pat was a Christian, so I asked her
about church.

'Oh,' she said, 'I'd love you to come along to my church on
Sunday. I don't go to the Santa Monica Vineyard though - I drive
up to Malibu if you don't mind giving that a try.' We didn't!

We felt very at home in the worship and the sermon was
incredible. When pastor Dave Owen spoke, it was so appropriate to our circumstances that it was as though he had been
briefed in advance of our visit. He taught on tragic circumstances and the most important thing being our response to the
situation.

I started to sense that it was not just for Joshua's sake that we
had made this trip. Dave's sermon was powerful and very helpful. It encouraged us that God was close with our pain and suffering and more than able to help us through it. I felt at home
immediately at the church and felt very close to God. We met

another of Pat's friends who also worked at Saint John's Hospital - 'Abecca' to our Joshua, who still had to master his 'r's and Rebecca got another person called Michael to pray for us after the service. These three were to become very significant friends.

A few days later, despite all my earlier misgivings, I had a strong conviction that we were right to come to America and that we would be coming back for a longer period. The impression I had was that our stay there was not just about Joshua's treatment at Saint John's Hospital, it was also for us to become part of the Malibu Vineyard church. I sensed God wanted to do something in us as a family during our time there. I also felt that we would meet stiff opposition about the prerequisite surgery back in London and that this feeling was God prompting me to stand firm with the medics. I would need to insist that the operation should go ahead to allow us the chance of getting on to Doctor Morton's vaccine. I was still not optimistic that the vaccine would work for Joshua, but I felt confident that we were in the right place and that we should at least give it a try. I believe God was confirming the 'rightness' of this trip to us by the Holy Spirit who, the Bible teaches, lives in us to comfort and guide us as we follow Jesus. I have rarely been so aware of His presence and guiding hand as I was just then.

We phoned through the news to GOS and a tentative date was scheduled for surgery, dependent on Professor Spitz seeing Joshua beforehand and reassessing the situation. Meanwhile, the tumours were on the rampage and we were distraught to see lumps, once shrunk by the chemo-immunotherapy, burgeoning in size again. Already we were dubious about Professor Spitz's willingness to operate and Coral was beginning to panic.

On the assumption that we would be coming back out for a

few months, I started to go on a fact-finding tour to find the
cheapest accommodation, car hire and information about the
cost of treatment in order to prepare. It was ironic that this time
I was more enthusiastic about organising our return than Coral.
I felt God was saying we would be back but perhaps the seriousness of stopping chemo-immunotherapy was only now catching
up with my wife. Her spirits were low and I could see the doubts
flooding in.

We were so anxious about the speed of regrowth of his
tumours that we decided to return to England as soon as possible and negotiate with the professor face to face for an earlier
operation.

During the flight home, I was even more dazzled by God's
goodness to us. I was just chuckling to myself that nothing
exceptional had happened on this last leg of the journey (other
than getting our much coveted bulkhead seats, bassinet for Misha
and mattress on the floor for Joshua once more) when, not even
knowing we were Christians, one member of the crew introduced himself to us. He was actually the steward in the business
class section of the plane, but had heard that a child with cancer
was travelling in economy class, so he came to introduce himself
and ask whether we would mind his church praying for Joshua.
We were delighted, of course and we exchanged addresses.

Back in London, it came as no surprise when the professor's
reaction to seeing Joshua again was less than positive. To be fair,
the lump had regrown almost to the size it was when we started
chemo-immunotherapy and it had been declared inoperable
then. It was devastating to watch but again we consoled ourselves that God WAS in control. The encouragements of our
American trip had left me in no doubt of that. I had to work hard

to persuade the doctors to operate.

'I would now say, at best I can only remove about 40% of the tumour,' the professor predicted. 'You know, even then it would be a very risky procedure to operate at all, so why bother?' After much prayer, fasting, persuasion and argument, the first signs of hope came when Professor Spitz agreed. 'I don't mind opening him up to remove the minimum tumour required to send the biopsy to the States.' Seizing this change of heart, I pushed again with, 'We would not want you to put our son at risk. We're not asking you to remove more than is safely feasible. We just feel very confident in your abilities. We're only asking that you do the best you can for him.' Finally, the negotiation paid off when the professor agreed to 'doing as much as is safely possible'.

I think it helped to see Joshua so vibrant, so well and so very alive despite the unimaginable traumas our boy had now been through in his short life. It was a miracle he could even enter a hospital without throwing a tantrum. Instead, it defied understanding that he loved and trusted the doctors and nurses as much as he loved and trusted everyone. Surely, this too was the work of God when naturally to him, hospital visits should have meant surgery and pain.

During our stay, I tried to find out as much as possible about fundraising. But God was not about to leave us in the lurch. Evidence of His help came on the day of the operation. Coral was in the Family Support office collecting a parking permit for me, when one of the workers received a phone call from a mother in the north of England. Coral's ears pricked up as the woman questioned her colleague. 'This lady on the phone has spare money available that they raised for their son. He had surgery in the States and they've paid for everything, with money left over that they don't need. She wants to help other parents who need medical treatment abroad but she doesn't know how to get in touch. Do we have a department in the hospital which deals with this?'

'Not really, there isn't a department for that specifically. Take her number and I'll call her back later.'

As she put the phone down, my wife could not hide her excitement.

'We need money to take our son to America for treatment. Would this person be interested in helping us?'

The same afternoon Coral found herself explaining Joshua's life history to 'the lady on the phone'. An hour later, we were promised the money for our flights and a further sum to cover some of our car hire.

Joshua's operation went ahead.

'Well, that was an outstanding success, though I say it myself!' exclaimed the professor as he visited Joshua post-operatively. 'I really have done an excellent job there. I've removed nearly all the tumour and still managed to close the wound. Of course, the closure doesn't look too neat. Your American doctors will probably not be impressed with the overstitching and nasty looking scar, but let's see if that's not sufficient for them. You'll have to wait for the drain to come out before you can leave. When are they expecting you back in the States?'

We were equally thrilled with what looked like a brilliant piece of very extensive surgery. Joshy himself was not so happy. He was hooked up in too many places for his liking and objected strongly to all the intravenous lines stuck into him.

By the time we left for home, our favourite airline had promised us that we could buy tickets for our medical travel at 'charity rate' - a considerable saving - and a friend of one of Joshua's favourite nurses, who also worked for the airline, had taken our details 'to see what he could do'.

Despite the grim pathology report that followed surgery, Doctor Morton said he would still honour our appointment to see for himself the possibility of the vaccine treatment. Again, there were no promises that Joshua would be accepted and no certainty that it would not be a wasted trip. If he was accepted, we knew that we could be asked to stay for two or three months and of course we had to organise for that possibility with my work and everything else. But instead of four days to prepare, this time we had just over a week before our appointment. We were becoming expert at hauling our family across the Atlantic at short notice and anyway this was the longest spell we had been able to enjoy at home in nearly four months.

As we packed again, Coral was still having doubts. She was sure that Joshua would be rejected, after all they had said to us in America before, but I was much more positive. I was busy setting up a fund to receive donations to help us finance a possible three-month stay and organising people to look after our personal affairs in England. We were both excited about going back to America and busy with all the preparations but Coral was losing heart as we watched the tumour starting to grow again within only a week of the operation. We both knew we had to go back one last time, even if only to finally satisfy ourselves that we had done everything we possibly could for Joshua.

'I can see no positive outcome for Joshua any more,' Coral struggled to tell me one evening. 'He won't be accepted onto the vaccine programme when we get there so why are we bothering with all this fund raising stuff?'

On the surface, she was right. Even after the surgery they were unlikely to accept us, but I just knew we were meant to return so I continued planning. It is hard to explain the feeling I had but I was utterly convinced God would take us back for a purpose. My hunch about what God had said about having to fight for the surgery had come true so I was even more confident now that the second part concerning our return to California would also happen. Once more the Lord helped us with so many of the practical arrangements, as 'coincidences' helped us find the best deals and travel companies bent over backwards to help us. The financial side was somewhat concerning. We had estimated that we would need some £18,000 for the first three months and a further £8000 - £10,000 for a year of monthly return trips to LA if the vaccine worked. We did not have that kind of ready money. All we had was a number of hopeful contacts with charities, but like every other issue we were facing, there was no time. We had one week. As I was now confident that we were in the will of God to return, the finance would be something we would have to rely on Him for. This too would be a new area of trust for us.

As arrangements again came together, the whole idea of relocating to the States seemed right on every count. Further confirmation came when my employers offered to let me take time off as necessary to stay in America on full pay for up to six months. Coral could not handle both children and all the medical decisions on her own, so I would be very much needed.

On my last day at work I met our oncology consultant for lunch to collect some more medical reports to take to the States. I decided not to tell Coral but he and I started talking about which palliative treatment options would be available when we returned to the UK and radiotherapy was mentioned. Jon wished us all well - he had become a good friend to us, but he admitted to me that we had pushed him further down the curative path for Joshua than he would have chosen to go without our influence.

So after another whirlwind of a week, we found ourselves packed for a three-month sojourn abroad. It seemed that the first chance we had to catch breath was when we were seated on the plane, back at 30,000 feet and heading west.

Chapter Eleven:

The generous side of California

Coral Recounts

We arrived at Los Angeles airport at 8 p.m. local time and were met by Pat Mullen, our friend at the hospital and church and her friend Mary. By now, Tim and Pat had spoken many times on the telephone and it was she who kindly organised a cot for Misha and even a bag full of groceries for our arrival at the same apartment as before. It was such a lovely welcome and a great relief not to have to spend an hour fussing around with car hire or shopping for essentials as soon as we got there with our tired little troupers - it had been seventeen hours since we left our house.

Everything was familiar to us second time around and it almost felt like coming home. Even our first night was an improvement on the previous visit, as Misha treated us to a little more sleep and even Joshua stayed in bed until a reasonable hour: well it was nearly 5 a.m. local time when he awoke the next morning!

'See Pitchard in Hopals?' Joshua asked us on our way in to the hospital. Poor Joshy was a bit confused that his English doctor would not be there. He was not disappointed though when the first person we met at the desk was 'Aunty Pat'. He remembered exactly which way to go as he ran out of the lift towards the desk. For us, it was a very nerve-racking appointment and we were gearing up to use all the powers of persuasion we possessed.

Pat was as keen as we were that Joshua should get accepted onto Doctor Morton's vaccine. She knew all the details and was praying as much as Tim and me that morning. As he caught sight of Joshua, Doctor Morton could not resist joining our meeting with his junior doctor and after a quick examination of the lumps he put his hand on his chin.

'Really, I don't hold out much hope. I have to be frank. If I had performed this surgery, I would have been more aggressive.' The deep hollow and long scar that was Joshua's neck looked pretty aggressive to us but before we said a word, he continued, 'The vaccine is not likely to cope with this amount of residual tumour. I admire your persistence in bringing him back here. He's a very friendly little fellow isn't he? I can see where he gets his stamina from!' Just as I was poised to plead our case, Doctor Morton continued, 'On the basis that you have no other treatment to turn to, I can't refuse him my vaccine. I'm declaring this an emergency situation and we'll get the necessary permission from the Committee next week. We need to start straight away. If you want to do this, you'll have to be prepared to let him have a lot of injections and to stay around a while though.'

I could hardly take in the rest of what he said as he explained the vaccine and the intensive programme he had selected for Joshua. The simple acceptance onto this treatment was so thrilling for us that we were ecstatic.

'He might be unwell for a day or so...' Elation coursed through our veins and the doctor's words seemed a blur. Joshua had been accepted on the programme. Meanwhile, Pat was hovering outside the room.

'What did he say?' she quizzed anxiously, but the relief on our faces and Tim's broad grin gave her the answer.

As usual Joshua was running around the corridors introducing himself to everyone. His top had been removed for the doctors to look at him but he had not a care in the world as he streaked around displaying his poorly scarred and birthmarked torso to many curious glances. There were a few shocked and sympathetic looks from some other patients but we were used to all that. How hard it was to even believe the seriousness of his condition when he was as lively and happy as this. He brought smiles to everyone as he hurtled in and out of rooms shouting 'Hi' and looking for people who would stop to entertain him. Perhaps he even picked up on our excitement. I could hardly believe that we were not being sent straight home after all. We would be staying in Santa Monica for at least the next two to three months.

I felt we were being given another chance, another drug that just might work. God had surely brought us to America; perhaps He would even heal him here.

We hurried home to telephone our family and friends in England and to discuss terms with our landlady.

It was not long before we received a telephone call from Pat at the hospital to enquire whether we would be prepared to allow the Channel 4 news station to do an article on Joshua. We learnt that the hospital wanted to support us as much as possible and would also like to set up an interview with the local newspaper to appeal to the community for help for us. At first we were a little nervous but we were talked around to the idea of an appeal which might help us to find more suitable accommodation and items necessary for such a long stay there with two small children. We were still extremely wary of media attention but Tim negotiated that everything would be handled through the hospital and our privacy respected.

Before we knew what was happening, there were more telephone calls from other staff in the hospital who wanted to get involved in our little project and they asked us for a list of everything we could use to make our stay more comfortable.

'Just make us a list!' the kind ladies from the fundraising department insisted. 'Everything you would go out and buy for yourselves or anything you would need to set up home here, just write it down. You have to hire a car? Right, put a car on the list.'

We felt like bashful children writing a Christmas list. It included a cheaper apartment, a car to borrow, toys for the children, an iron and so on. When we returned to the hospital, only five days since our arrival, we were met by the television camera and requests to film Joshua's vaccination.

It was quite a surprise to us to return to our apartment that afternoon and see ourselves already on the television as part of a trailer for news that was still to come. As we returned to the hospital, not only were there the cameraman, newsreader and his assistant waiting for us, but we were also met by newspaper reporters all at the same time. We hardly knew which way to turn first and were somewhat overwhelmed. We proceeded with the filming and then went on to the press interview. By this time, Joshua was understandably bored and one of the hospital staff took him off in the lift to the hospital shop. Some minutes later they reappeared with a bag full of brand new toys donated by the manager of the shop. Joshua had obviously chosen them as each one made a noise or had flashing lights! He was happy again and entertained us all as we answered the reporters' questions.

The schedule was put together for his treatment which also included weekly blood samples from his Hickman Line and bi-weekly vaccinations and skin tests. The vaccinations themselves were a little more than we bargained for, as they involved eight separate jabs at once all around his stomach, as well as three smaller jabs on his arm for the skin tests. Even Joshua, with his wonderful resilience to needles, found this understandably intolerable and objected strongly. As he screamed and nurses and patients gave us such sympathetic looks, I wondered if I was becoming a little immune to seeing our son hurting. At the same time I knew that as soon as it was over he would immediately recover and urged everyone to perform their tasks as quickly as possible. It was useless trying to calm him down if he knew there was more to come and it only prolonged the episode, so the kindest thing was just to 'go for it' and get it over with. I'm sure some people must have thought we were being hard on him as his screaming seemed to be so traumatised but he really did bounce back the second it was finished.

As soon as we were featured on Channel 4 News and then in the local newspaper, the telephone started ringing. This time it was not other reporters wanting to do a story (except for the Los Angeles Times who were keen to pay us a visit if we wanted), but offers of help. There were a number of apartments to investigate and even one or two offers of rooms within a home rent free. One offer was from a local businesswoman, a little bungalow rent free close to the hospital and just three blocks away from the beach. The location was idyllic.

'Everybody wants to help you,' said our potential landlady, Gwen. 'I have friends and family waiting to donate china and cutlery and I have all the baby equipment you need as our little

Christina is just growing out of it all now. We can probably get
you a television and everything if you give us a couple of weeks.
I'm sure it will all come together.' The generosity was almost
overwhelming and we kept waiting for the catch, but it got even
more unbelievable as she continued, 'The carpets are not great
but don't worry, I'll have them all cleaned for you and you can
come to my house and choose which sofa you prefer. Oh yes, a
rocking chair, you must have one for feeding the baby in the
night and we can get her a bassinet (carry cot) too. Just leave it
all to me.'

Gwen's enthusiasm was infectious and we could not help
warming to this incredibly generous lady. We were stunned and
found it hard to take in. It was just what we needed.

Meanwhile, as though in competition with each other, the
hospital staff and other Californians responding to the local
paper astounded us with their generosity. There was such a stack
of toys and equipment accumulating at the hospital that a daily
visit there became necessary for a while. Tim went to collect 'a
few things' and returned home with a car load of toys, baby
walker, bouncer, ironing board and all sorts of household good-
ies. We could hardly believe our eyes. There was even a car to
be made available to us shortly for a month or so, a Mercedes no
less, saving us the expense of car hire for a while!

The day we moved into our little home in Third Street will
always stick in our minds for the thrill of what we found there.
The place was transformed. Not only did they get every room
cleaned and fitted out for us in a week as Gwen had promised,
but they even had it painted, had taken doors off hinges and fitted safety features for the children even down to the guards on
all the power sockets. It simply blew our minds. There were

fresh flowers, pictures on the wall, beautiful crockery, candles in the lounge, toys in a toy box and every cupboard in the kitchen full of kitchen and dining ware. A fun rollaway bed was made up for Joshua, there were more toys in the bath and a beautiful bassinet for Misha complete with musical mobile. The thoughtfulness of Gwen and Bruce was truly inspirational. We walked around from room to room with our mouths wide open as we explored and discovered the perfect details in every corner. There was even a travel cot in the closet for when Misha grew out of her little bed.

How could we ever thank these people? I was at a loss as to how to express such gratitude and amazement and all I could do was shed more tears.

Joshua ran in and made straight for his favourite item. 'Ooooh phone!' he exclaimed, 'I press a number!' as he picked up the receiver and started to push the digits. The plug was swiftly pulled and we employed our usual distraction tactics to tempt him away. As we settled in, still the gifts kept arriving. A toaster, an iron, a fan and anything we could possibly use was turning up day after day with Bruce our landlord as delivery man. He was even seen to put up a swing in the little yard for Joshua. All of this was their own idea and their Mexican handyman 'Gregorio', or 'Goro' as Joshua preferred to call him, was at our little home with his paintbrush or tool set for at least a month full-time, putting all the finishing touches to the outside. Joshua missed nothing and greeted 'Goro' on every visit.

One day, Tim was again asked at the hospital what people could do to help us or what could be provided and he jokingly suggested a laptop computer was all he needed now. Within a week even that was loaned to us, so we started using it to write our epic 'Joshua letters'. By now we were sending out nearly two hundred letters and with everything happening so fast in America we resorted to a monthly mailing to keep everyone advised. I am sure that so many people praying for us across the world contributed significantly to the blessings we were experiencing in California. Materially we were blessed beyond our wildest dreams and spiritually too, God was touching us in a new way that caused us to feel very peaceful and totally dependent upon Him.

For church life, we went back to the Malibu Vineyard, which Pat had introduced us to in February and we continued to enjoy the preaching and worship. It quickly became our 'spiritual home' during our stay and as the congregation learned of our reason for being there, many offers of prayer and practical help were made to us. We in turn opened our home to some of the single people there, inviting them to feel welcome to visit any time, with or without an invitation. We remembered only too well how lonely being single can be at times. We were enjoying getting to know them as well as appreciating their faithfulness in praying for us regularly too. It was not long before Joshua adopted 'Abecca', Pat and Michael as his firm friends.

After a few enquiries, the hospital introduced us to a pre-school next door and Joshua was signed up for two mornings a week, again with the hospital paying or waiving the charge. It would replace his playgroup at home and give him the social contact he needed with children his own age. It meant one of us staying with him but there was something really positive about watching him play and just do normal things with other children. Of course there were differences as he had to be well covered from the sun at playtime and occasionally another child would make remarks about Joshua's skin. Thankfully, he was always running around too fast to take much notice and it was left for me to explain discreetly to them while he bolted away to the next exciting activity.

I'm sure the other children's reactions were more of a problem to me than to him and although I managed to put on a brave face, I still remember sitting out in the playground and fighting back the tears on occasions. One day, he discovered the water butt and a few toys that could be played with in the water. He made a little game of filling a saucepan, carrying it carefully across the sand and watering a tree. I watched quietly from a distance as I saw another child start to copy him and then another, until there were about five of them in all going in a line between the water butt and the tree. It was such a special moment because until that time he had been playing mostly alone. The other children had already made their little friends and I was becoming increasingly concerned to see Joshua not being fully accepted into their groups. He had found friends among the adult teachers and helpers so it perturbed me more than him, but this day it was as though his 'great idea' had won him favour in the eyes of his peers and now he was accepted and even leading them. I had to wipe tears from my eyes again as I observed my brave little captain shouting his instructions and enjoying his life to the full. He was smaller than the other children but again, seemingly oblivious to the fact. We had always liked to believe that his character would win him friends and here was the evidence I needed.

It was impossible to keep Joshua occupied indoors for long so there were mini excursions to the beach in the evening from time to time or trips to the shopping mall. He loved to be out and enthusiastically pointed out to us planes, boats and everything else he spotted. His powers of observation often amazed us as he noticed and enjoyed so much of the surroundings that we constantly take for granted, or do not even notice. Having both of us around, he took to calling us by our Christian names, to the amusement of many of our friends. 'Tim, Cowol, need help!' was a constant shout whenever he got frustrated or stuck on something and his 'Uh oh, in touble,' has become a family watchword and continues to make us laugh.

Already a month had passed since our arrival. The tumours were growing fast again and causing Joshua's neck and jaw line to become quite distended. There was such a swelling that an emergency appointment was booked with Doctor Morton. Even then, he was not sure whether the swelling was a positive reaction to the vaccine and therefore a good thing or whether it was increasing tumour mass in spite of the vaccine. Only time would tell.

Easter crept up on us and we were invited up to Rancho Cucamonga to spend the holidays with Dave and Vivien Cunningham, their parents, children and grandchildren. When we joined Dave's church for Sunday morning we were overwhelmed by the love that greeted us. Dave introduced us at the front and it was that many of the congregation had been following our story since Joshua's birth. They gathered around us to pray and hardly a person was left seated or with dry eyes afterwards. It was a level of emotion we were not used to seeing so publicly displayed in England but somehow it was very comforting and beautiful to see the love in the eyes of people who had never even met us before.

Not only were we being blessed in America, but also in

England. I shall never forget the day when Tim casually asked our friend Sue on the phone how the 'Joshua Fund' was faring. When we had left the UK, there were only a few thousand pounds in it and we had already used a great deal. I hadn't believed at the time that we would ever stay long on this second visit so I had not been that worried about the small amount of money in the face of such a large anticipated total expense. Tim was more concerned, yet so confident that the return to California was for several months and part of God's plan for our family. That my normally conservative husband was willing to take this huge financial risk in spite of his worries was evidence that he, too, was changing.

'Oh there is fifteen or sixteen thousand,' Sue said casually. After Tim had picked himself up from the floor we were amazed to hear how the money was flowing in. It was remarkable how God was providing for us. We were very humbled to hear the stories from Sue of just how friends and acquaintances, the companies that relatives worked for, other charities and local businesses were all responding to our situation. We were deeply, deeply touched and felt indebted even to complete strangers whom we had never met. A similar thing was happening for us in California too, with complete strangers still donating things to equip our temporary home and donating finances to cover our medical needs, or even just so that we could afford to spoil Joshua a bit whilst in America. We were left speechless at the amazing provision. The Bible talks a lot about God providing for our every need and here we were seeing that first hand. Underneath it all we were learning new levels of trusting God.

It is very easy to think that you are 'trusting God' for everything when you have a regular pay cheque and roughly enough money to meet the bills, as we always did before. The real test came for us when we faced a big discrepancy between what we could see coming in and what we needed. Yet we saw first hand that if God has called us to do something, He will provide exactly what we need and will use incredible means to do so.

And my God will meet all your needs according to His glorious riches in Christ Jesus.[31]

---

[31] *Philippians 4 v 19*

Chapter Twelve:

Happiest and hardest times

Coral Recounts

The summer was hotting up in Santa Monica and so too was our pace of life. Whatever happened with our son, we wanted to ensure that he had the best quality of life we could give him. It was even more important if his time was to be short. Joshua himself was still wonderfully oblivious to the heartache we were facing on his behalf. His happy outlook constantly reminded us to make the most of his life, so we just decided to have fun with him and did so! Life was rising to a dizzy crescendo as we crammed every day with relentless 'child-focused' activity. My 'block it out and get on with life' mentality meant this was easier for me than it was for my husband, but even there I believe God had a hand in helping Tim to make the most of what we had. It was simply not in his nature to smile and put on a brave face in the midst of such pain. Yet, smile he did and worship like never before. Life had built up again to a peak of business and intensity, but somehow in the middle of this we actually found ourselves drawing close to God again. We could hardly wait for Sundays when we could really express our worship. We were organising excursions to Disneyland and the like one day and serious hospital appointments the next. Such fun, such fear and such extremes.

Just then I would have called myself optimistic but perhaps a better description would have been 'in denial'. I could not cope with any more downward lunges. We needed God's wisdom more than ever. We were living on such mixed levels both individually and as a couple. In our hearts we both expected Joshua to die at some point but neither of us could face that fully at this stage. Tim still wanted to live in hope that God might yet work a miracle. I shut out the thoughts of death by only living for the day and not looking too far ahead.

We did not doubt God's ability to heal Joshua directly and miraculously, or even instantaneously. We even pushed ourselves to carry on looking to Him to intervene. Whether Joshua got healed or not, we believed, was down to the sovereign will of God alone. There was nothing that we could add to His power. We endeavoured to keep our focus on Him and not get hung up about what was within us. We knew we were somewhat emotional. We had no internal reserves of strength remaining, yet in this place we reached a deeper trust in our Lord than we would have thought possible. Whether we are 'in faith' or 'in fear' God is sovereign and we knew then as we know now that we could trust His greater wisdom, without needing to understand it fully. If God allowed Joshua to die, it was not a failing on our part. Until such time we would still pray for his healing and take advantage of any opportunity for others to do this also.

Just when our lives were reaching this hectic peak, we heard of an imminent televised meeting with evangelist Benny Hinn only two hours away in Anaheim. Our resourceful friend Pat soon fixed it for us all to go there and even arranged for us to receive personal prayer from Benny at the end of the meeting. We had seen many of the incredible healing miracles that had occurred during his meetings on the Christian television channel. The extravaganza of lights, suspended TV monitors and loud music mesmerised both Misha and Joshua. Even though there were many obviously sick people there, the sight of our blood-stained little warrior and his hideously contused neck was clear-ly shocking to others. It was so clear to anyone that Joshua had an excruciating and grotesque problem, but for us it was still hard to look at this cute energetic character and think of his life expiring. To watch his ecstatic delight in all manner of circum-stances was all-engrossing. While others around us were repulsed by the ugly tumours, our concern was mainly for the effect their repulsion might have on our precious little boy. At one point during worship one of the television personalities, Steve Brock, walked past us, then did a double take and came back, putting his hands on our shoulders and praying for us spon-taneously. Joshua closed his eyes to pray and repeated our thank you to this godly man, who was clearly one of many who was instantly moved and appreciative of our little boy's response to him.

After the service, we waited patiently outside Benny's room for prayer. Benny came straight towards us and started praying. With heartfelt compassion he simply said, 'Don't give up, just don't give up.'

He made his way down the line of others waiting and then paused on his way past us again to repeat his earlier comment - 'Just don't give up.'

As it turned out, Benny Hinn's words became quite significant to us later that week when we were called back from Anaheim to an unexpected meeting with Doctor Morton. By now the lumps on Joshua's jaw, neck and even his collar bone had regrown hor-rendously. It was perhaps even bigger than before we had taken him home for the operation, so when we arrived, the shocked reaction of the hospital staff should have come as no surprise to us. We were so used to seeing this type of rapid growth over the years that we forgot how alarming it was and we were unprepared for what the doctor had to tell us. Joshua was in serious trouble.

'My personal opinion is that you should give up and take him home. I would say that the tumour is now doubling in size every four to ten days and the vaccine treatment does not stand a chance of halting it. Without surgery, Joshua will soon be unable to swallow,' Doctor Morton advised. 'It would be a very serious operation and even IF it succeeded without severing a major artery, there would certainly be facial paralysis on one side. If I were you, I would book the next flight home.'

We could see for ourselves the size of growths but he was otherwise healthy and beginning to really enjoy California. Surely the doctor would not think like that if he had seen him only hours earlier squealing with delight in Minnie Mouse's house or 'driving' the motorised racing car around the track. We were not ready to accept defeat and take him home. With Benny Hinn's words fresh in our minds we asked what else could be done.

Just one final option might remain and that was to attempt Gamma radiation treatment twice a week, which could specifically target just the tumours. After further discussion and reassurance, a provisional booking was made for the following morning.

It was a particularly difficult night. We both felt very shocked and consumed with what we had heard and were not agreed about which course of action to take. Tim instinctively did not want the radiation treatment, whereas I did not want surgery.

'I can't bear to think of Joshy with a permanent 'drop face'. And who knows how long it will be before the tumour regrows?' I protested. 'He's already had two major operations on his neck and the cancer has still regrown hideously. Why run the risk again?' Tim did not entirely agree. He was thinking more long term than I was.

'Yes, but what's worse? If radiation works, but they hit his bone, that bone will stop growing and he will have years of reconstruction surgery throughout his childhood and adolescence and into adulthood. Surely the disfigurement of a jaw and neck bones frozen at the size of a three-year-old's will look far worse than a drop face. Plus, we know people who are facing immense problems now because they received radiation treatment earlier in life. Even the radiologist said that the risk of secondary cancers from radiation is greater in twenty or thirty years time.'

Neither option was attractive. A phone call to Sylvia Owen, the Malibu church pastor's wife, resulted in people at church praying that we would get specific wisdom and agree on our decision. Making these choices was so excruciating and it felt too much for us on our own.

It was the lesser of two evils in the end - we decided to go with the radiation. There was a lot of hanging around the next morning as all the equipment had to be moved into a room specially for Joshua's radiotherapy. Then we watched our little anaesthetised boy on the closed circuit TV monitor, lying on a table under this great big machine which delivered such powerful rays that could damage as much as they could cure. Afterwards, with everything organised for the next dose the following Monday, we returned to Disneyland and tried to put on a

brave face for Joshua's sake. As we entered the park mid afternoon we were just in time for the parade and Joshua's excitement
soon brought smiles to our faces.

We returned to Santa Monica and I stared at my beautifully
prepared calendar of family outings, which was now redundant.
Then I reasoned with myself that it had, after all, become our
lifestyle to cancel plans or simply live life without any. The disappointment of aborting my schedule for medical treatment was
nothing new.

At the weekend, Pat Mullen had arranged for us to meet John
Wimber at his home church back in Anaheim. It was just a normal Sunday evening service at the Vineyard's headquarters where
John was speaking but we were still a little nervous about meeting this man. His reputation of being such a godly person made
us feel somewhat abashed. For Joshua's sake though, we would
approach anyone. Again, nothing obvious happened when John
prayed for Joshua after the service but we enjoyed such a positive
experience, sharing with John and his wife Carol in their room
backstage. Something of the majesty yet humility of Jesus met us
that night in John and Carol. We felt unexpectedly at ease with
them, even while Joshua ran around in his usual fashion of a train
that never stops. We sat, talked, prayed and listened and knew
we were understood. We were not alone in our hurting and pain
and importantly, even if we were not confident that God was
going to heal Joshua in this world, we were not condemned.
After all, if it depended entirely on our 'faith', we would be
reducing God the Almighty Creator to being our personal pup-
pet. Sometimes Christians seem to talk about 'faith for healing'
in a way that implies that whilst they recognise God's ability to
heal miraculously, it depends on the quantity of 'faith' they can

muster. If they have a certain amount of it, God will do something and if they don't have quite enough of it, He won't. So often, this can lead us into condemnation. Jesus Himself said that one only needed a tiny amount (mustard seed) to move mountains. There is the sin of unbelief and without faith it is impossible to please God. But these two truths are about where our focus is: God and His ability, or ourselves and ours.

It was another opportunity for God to take away Joshua's disease in a dramatic way. Like Benny Hinn, John Wimber was no stranger to praying for the sick and seeing miracles before his eyes. Although physically Joshua appeared no different for all this anointed prayer, we did not regret for a moment that we had been so privileged to have met these men. It gave us the comfort that we had sought out every option, both medically and spiritually, for our son.

Monday morning arrived and this meant the next radiotherapy. After the first treatment Joshua and Tim went on their own. He would lift him out of his bed and into the car at 8 a.m. twice a week without fully waking him. By the time he realised he was up for the day, they were in the Radiation department and there was Aunty Carol, the receptionist, Doctor Kenny Sachs, the anaesthetist and John the radiographer to greet them. Joshua would rush around saying 'hi' to everyone enthusiastically, not once pausing to ask for breakfast.

The effect of a general anaesthetic on Joshua was very slight. By now he had had over forty of them in his life of as many months and he recovered remarkably fast. Even so, there was a side-effect of fatigue from the radiation which we were not used to seeing in our energy-filled son.

'Joshla just restin,' became a frequent rebuttal to our encouragements to walk or play.

I was feeling hopeful again as radiation began though. If the treatment could first shrink the tumours, the vaccine might have a chance I reasoned, even after the first couple of sessions when Ken, the radiologist expressed some concern and increased the radiation dose. There was talk as well of going to three sessions a week, but that never happened. It soon became clear that Joshua was not in the 80% of patients to see a rapid response to radiation, as sessions three and four passed and the decision was taken to continue for longer still. The skin around his neck began to ulcerate and we were concerned about infection but it did not change my resolve to show Joshua a good time. So we planned a short break.

We booked a hotel on the island of Catalina for a night and took the ferry over. What really appealed about this place was that it's tiny size meant that most people there drive around in golf carts rather than cars. In fact, there were no taxis or hire cars on Catalina and very few cars are even allowed to be taken there by the residents. This trip was as much for our benefit as Joshua's so we delighted in our beautiful room overlooking the ocean. Tim and I enjoyed a romantic evening when the children even treated us by both going to sleep early. Perhaps it was the family jacuzzi we had in our room just before their bed time, or the sound of the lapping waves which put them into sleepland. Either way, the tranquillity was so removed from busy Los Angeles that we could fully understand why it was such a popular spot with the LA locals. There was something utterly relaxing and therapeutic about escaping to this place and we could almost feel our batteries recharging. It was also the perfect retreat for us to pause and take stock of all that was happening.

After the bath that evening Joshua had climbed into Misha's cot and was having fun tickling her. It was perhaps a little rougher than we would have liked but as usual he was making her laugh. His neck touched the sheet and a few spots of blood stood out against the white. A slightly nervous Joshua pointed it out to us with, 'Oooh, a bit a bud Mummy!' But he was easily reassured by the reply, 'Oh yes, a bit of blood, never mind.'

His movement was a little restricted as we noticed he could not turn his head fully to the left anymore, but we never heard a single complaint or anything which confirmed he was even bothered by this discomfort. He was conscious of his body, as occasionally he would point to a birthmark on his hand or arm and remark, 'spot' or even, 'birthmark' in a somewhat sad or pensive way but it was forgotten within seconds. The only time he mentioned his neck was in conjunction with asking Jesus to 'make sore neck better' in our nightly prayers. Could it be that God was protecting him from the impact of this grotesque disease and enabling him to enjoy life fully as though there was nothing there? Certainly, it seemed like a miracle to us and again no coincidence that so many hundreds and possibly thousands were praying for our little boy across the world.

For Tim and me, it tore at our emotions to see such hideous and ugly deformities on the son we loved so deeply. At times we loathed, hated those tumours with a vengeance for their destructive presence in Joshua's body. It pained us to see other children and sometimes other adults recoil at the ugliness of the disease. There were fewer curious comments now but this was only because the condition had become so obviously serious.

And yet, as Tim remarked occasionally, these too were just other aspects of the way Joshua's life could illustrate the gospel.

God the Father felt the same revulsion in far greater measure about the sin in our lives. He could not tolerate man's disease, to the extent that He allowed His only Son to die so that man could receive the only remedy possible for his own deeply ingrained disease called sin. Man's sinful nature can only be healed by the shed blood of Jesus. What father would choose death for a son? It can only be that God's immense love for all mankind drove Him to such lengths in order to provide the only means possible to heal our deadly disease.

> *For God so loved the world that He gave His one and only Son, that whoever believes in Him shall not perish but have eternal life.*[32]

Jesus also faced rejection, as described in the book of Isaiah, chapter 53.[33] We thought we were facing tough things on behalf of Joshua and yet when we thought about it, God the Father and Jesus went through similar things in far greater measure.

Back in Catalina the highlight for Joshua was probably the semi-submerged boat trip which gave us a guided water safari. In the bottom half of the vessel it felt just like being in a submarine and the guide pointed out the fish and plant life as we made our way around part of the island. With each of us sitting on either side of the boat and windows all around Joshua ran back and forth shouting, 'Look Tim! Look Cowol! Wow! Cor!' in his usual uninhibited manner. Other passengers seemed amused and, thankfully, not too annoyed by his excitement. When the

---

[32] *John 3 v 16* [33] *Isaiah 53 v 3: "He was despised and rejected by men, a man of sorrows, and and familiar with suffering. Like one from whom men hide their faces, he was despised and we esteemed him not."*

guide asked if there were any questions towards the end of the trip, nobody answered and then, bold as brass, Joshua replied loudly and directly to her, 'Yeah, I see fishy!' and continued the conversation with, 'A big one!' as though he had been the first person in the world to make the discovery and was desperate to share it with everyone.

'Well good. That's what we hoped you would see,' the lady replied. Everyone laughed.

Although Joshua seemed to enjoy the ride, there were signs that day which began to worry us that all was not well with him. He was fretting and unhappy for no obvious reason and we started to suspect that he might be suffering some pain. So began a somewhat confusing time. Some days there would seem to be nothing wrong at all and Joshua was incredibly happy, his usual buoyant self in fact, but then there were days when he would be difficult to please and we always wondered if it was normal toddler development, tiredness or something much more sinister causing his upset. In every case he would cheer up again, usually after a good nap, so we preferred to believe the best.

There was no getting away from the obvious growth though. Unfortunately there was no hiding it either as it was predominately above collar level. The special caps he always wore with a protective back flap were becoming too short to hide the growing mass and several of his tops were impossible to pull over his head. I had to dress him in shirts and leave top buttons undone but if the wind was blowing, the 'legionnaire's' flap on his hat had to be tucked down inside the shirt collar to keep it in place. This was another area we had always had to be strong with him about so he was used to keeping on a hat whenever we ventured outside. Then we ran into another problem as the tumour also began growing badly under his chin and the elastic from the hats cut a groove in the swollen mass. I found myself sewing in longer and longer elastic. I reassured myself that at least the cancer was growing outwards, rather than growing inwards and affecting his breathing and swallowing. All of this change was over a matter of days and weeks. It was clear that even with radiation, the vaccine was not holding the disease.

It was hard to keep him cool and still protect every area of his skin from the sunshine and people's stares, but even worse, the lumps started to bleed again as they did when he was first born. However hard I tried to protect our little man from the curious stares of strangers, there was no escaping the obvious blood stains which appeared nearly every day, seeping through the extra lightweight material. It had to be a miracle that Joshua himself was still the most self-confident little fellow, utterly secure and totally oblivious to the intrusive looks of those around him.

We were enjoying another few days away when we were next called back to see Doctor Morton for a consultation that shattered the expectation we had of the future. He was not at all happy with the way Joshua's cancer was raging. We were reminded that the CT scan with the first dose of radiation had revealed that tumours were pressing on Joshua's windpipe and that they were some 5 cm thick in places. Left unchecked, we were told they would simply strangle him. We were back to the days of going to hospital and coming away physically nauseated with the shock of what we were being told. This was also a new interpretation of what course the disease might take. Up until now we had been led to believe that the tumours would continue to grow outwards and away from his windpipe. We had expected that the cancer might eventually spread to his vital organs, but through consistently praying for the purity of his blood, this had not happened for over three years. While he remained so healthy, we thought that we still had time. After all, we had always been advised that melanoma kills through secondary cancers in a vital organ, typically the brain, lungs or liver. We had never liked seeing these gross tumours disfiguring Joshua's face and neck, but we did not realise that the cancer could kill him from that position. Suddenly, the buffer zone between the present condition and the final prelude before likely death evaporated. This was it, medically speaking. There would be no discovery of secondaries, no final blasts of treatment to save his liver or lung or brain and no time for us to adjust and prepare. The disease was already poised and the moment had caught us unaware.

When we got home we phoned Sylvia Owen again at the Malibu Vineyard and she activated the church's 'prayer chain' once more on our behalf. It meant so much to us that people who barely knew us were prepared to spend time praying to God on our behalf. Tim needed this support more than ever as his heart was absolutely breaking. Perhaps mine would have been too, if I had allowed myself to accept the gravity of Joshua's predicament.

As usual, I busied myself. My boy particularly still needed entertaining. So in the middle of all this I organised yet another excursion, this time taking Rebecca with us to San Diego for a few days. "While we are here, we should take Joshua and Misha to see SeaWorld," I reasoned and they loved it. For those few days we had a totally wonderful time - a brief respite to keep us sane. A very special moment came for us after the dolphin show, when we were taken back stage and Joshua was allowed to stroke the dolphins. He was thrilled to bits.

'Oooh, Fishy mummy,' he exclaimed as he bent forward to touch the prostrate dolphin at his feet. 'Big fishy!' My grip on Misha in the baby sling tightened and as I looked at Tim I noticed his eyes were filling up like mine to see Joshua's innocent wonder and joy. It surprised me that such happy times with our boy would occasionally make me feel as emotional as the hard times did. This tender moment illuminated for me the intense pain that had engulfed our family. I also noticed Joshua was tiring even more. We found ourselves wondering how long radiation would have to continue and how long it would take for him to recover from his exhaustion once it was complete. It did not occur to me that he would not recover. This was our little warrior and he always did.

Chapter Thirteen:
The end of the medical journey - choosing life
Tim Recounts

'It seems Joshua is not responding at all to the radiation,' Doctor Morton told us on our next appointment. We had already noticed new lumps were growing on the right side of his neck and jaw - the opposite side to the radiation treatment. 'You should pack up and go home to England while Joshua is still well enough to travel,' he continued.

This prompted us to ask the ultimate question of how much time he thought Joshua had left.

'From my experience, I would say fifty, plus or minus thirty, days. During that time the tumour will strangle his windpipe. In any case, he will soon need hospitalisation and palliative care.'

We could not speak. The impact of this prediction jarred us, as his words so often did of late. If Doctor Morton was right, that meant Joshua might die in three weeks time - or at most, only had under three months to live. It was too unbearable to count his time in days as the doctor did. It was Thursday 16th May, 1996.

A clock started ticking in my mind.

Ken the radiologist was more positive about continuing longer with the radiation and although Coral was relieved to learn this, I could not help wondering if he just did not have the heart to tell us what he really thought. The staff at the hospital had become emotionally involved with our valiant little man and they were struggling with the idea that the only child they had treated in a long time looked increasingly like he might not make it. I too was struggling with this realisation but Coral would not allow herself such negative thoughts just yet. It was all too sudden for her - she was avoiding hitting the wall at 100 mph. It was too much of a shock to withdraw Joshua's treatment there and then. Surely, if we radiated the right side now as well as the left she reasoned...

Doctor Morton was very surprised that Joshua was still so active and even more surprised that he was having no trouble in eating or drinking. His description of Joshua's condition did not fit with the lively boy in front of us all so his advice to return home just did not feel right either. There were times when Joshua was clearly exhausted but in the next couple of hours he could be running as wild as ever, bossing everyone about with his constant instructions and not missing a trick. It was such a confusing time with emotions and reason running at conflicting levels. Underneath it all I realised that we were coming to the end of the medical journey. But what was God saying in all this? How should we approach things practically?

It was true that Joshua's breathing was beginning to get noisy. We had noticed that he had started to make snoring noises and wheezes in his sleep and that was a new development. His little bed was in the closet off our own bedroom and since the talk with Doctor Morton I could not ignore what I was hearing as I tried to sleep each night. Fear would grip me in the silence of the night.

'I want to take him home alive. I want our families to see him again,' I asserted in my prayers. My grieving for him was already beginning and yet we had to hear what God was saying about all this. More than ever I was convinced that God could heal Joshua without medical intervention. I was convinced that God had given the medics such wisdom in handling Joshua's rare case for over three years. Conventional medical practice for melanoma had proved useless in curing Joshua's cancer since he was only six months old. Yet, here we were rearing a lively toddler against all odds. God had been so good to us in that. Our lives had been enriched and utterly changed by this precious character. 'How we have learned so much more about You God and seen You do fantastic things in our family. What should we do now?' I knew that we would have to go home soon, but it just did not feel right to rush home in a panic.

'Well, what was the last clear direction God gave to you?' Dave Cunningham asked as we had lunch at our favourite pasta restaurant on Montana Avenue. Again Dave and Vivien were there for us when we most needed them and their advice was always sound. 'From what I remember you saying when you first arrived, you felt that you should stay here for as long as the hospital were prepared to treat Joshua and for as long as he would get the better care here in California than is available back home in England. Have those criteria changed?' Coral and I glanced at each other and shook our heads. 'Well, in the absence of a new signpost pointing out a new direction, stick with the direction you last felt God speak clearly to you about. Let's pray that the peace of God comes to you.'

It made eminent sense and a weight lifted from my shoulders. The hospital was prepared still to provide the radiation treatment. The routine here was very slick and the least traumatic for Joshua. We had no idea what the cost of all this would be, but that did not feature in our consideration at this point. Coral and I resolved to pray independently that God would make clear to us which date we should choose to travel home on.

After a couple of days Coral and I both felt the end of May was the date to return home. She seemed perfectly at ease trusting God would work it out, but something was bothering me and I was still not entirely peaceful.

That night I went to the home group led by Felix and Nancy Schmittdiel from the Malibu Vineyard. When I arrived I was broken. Then, God in His goodness met with me powerfully as we worshipped. The Bible is true in what it says about God's 'grace' - that His strength is there to help in time of need; just as that midwife's tea mug had reminded me on the very day Joshua was born. Saint Paul writes in his letter to the Corinthian church:

> *To keep me from becoming conceited...there was given me a thorn in my flesh...to torment me. Three times I pleaded with the Lord to take it from me. But He said to me 'My grace is sufficient for you, for My power is made perfect in weakness'. Therefore I will boast all the more gladly about my weakness so that Christ's power may rest on me.* [34]

The realisation had struck home to me that I could not 'fix' Joshua's cancer. As men we are used to fixing things for our families. As a husband and father I expect to provide and care for my wife and children, to fix things when they break, to do the DIY (albeit grudgingly!).

Our resolute drive to find a cure, to choose life for our son, had driven us ultimately 5000 miles around the globe to live in a

---

[34] *2 Corinthians 12 v 7 - 9*

foreign country, put my career to one side for an indefinite period of time, incur large medical and living expenses with no clear idea where the money would come from and all of this with a three-month-old baby girl as well. Then it hit me. However proud I felt of our achievements so far, I could not cure Joshua. I could not do a thing. This desire for life for my son was beyond my natural abilities as a man and as his father to provide. I fell short and it cut me up. I wept from the guts.

Suddenly but gently, the sweet realisation dawned afresh and in a deeper way that where I could not, God could. What I could not fix, God could. Where I was weak, God was strong. A renewed trust in His ability surged into my pain, coupled with a sense of excitement that now all other sources of provision had been declared bankrupt and all other avenues for a cure had failed or were failing. There was one mighty player left on the stage - God and God alone. What would He choose for my boy? He alone would decide. Not the disease, not other players, not even us as his parents.

'Lord, it is now down to You and You alone,' I prayed. Here was a new depth of surrender to God's sovereignty, a new place of trust for Him to determine our future. The whole theme of trust and surrender to God that Abraham displayed in offering his son Isaac as a sacrifice flashed through my mind once more.

As the home group continued, I felt God the Holy Spirit refresh and restore me immensely. When the group came to pray the weight and flow of prophetic encouragement towards me and my family's future was immense. I was blown away, as one after the other, people said specific things which confirmed words brought by other individuals over the preceding months and years. Once more a weighty sense of destiny and purpose struck me: everything that was happening to my family and me was part of God's bigger picture for our lives.

Back home that night, Joshua's breathing seemed particularly noisy as I tried to sleep. I had such a swirl of fears and thoughts, following such a powerful time with God at the home group.

Doubts returned over breakfast the next day and I quizzed Coral once more.

'Are we really doing the right thing, waiting until the end of May before returning? I really want our families to see him alive one more time. Can we really leave it that long? Will he be well enough to travel in two weeks' time?'

'Well, we both did pray and that was the date we both felt God had ringed for us. I'm sure God wouldn't let us down and have him die in flight after all we've come through.'

'Yes but…' I thought, 'you're not facing the reality of Joshua's deterioration.' And she wasn't.

Joshua was running around in his nappy and the little 'tubi-grip' top, which held his Hickman Line against his torso out of harm's way. In such a state of undress, there was no ignoring the hideous mess the tumours were making of his neck and the extensive brown birthmarks covering his back and limbs. It was a warm Saturday morning and the back door was open onto the yard shared with our neighbours. I heard Joshua greet someone from the back doorstep.

It was the gas man, coming to do something to our neighbour's meter. Conscious of Joshua's appearance, I went to the back door to call him inside and acknowledged the gas man. A few seconds later he was back at our gate, calling for me.

'Sir, I just had to come back. It is obvious that your son has problems. Would you mind if I prayed for you. I believe that nothing is impossible for God.'

'No, not at all,' I replied, holding Joshua in my arms. 'We're Christians too.'

Daniel's already radiant face broke out into a broad smile.

'Why that's wonderful. When I saw you call your son inside, I just couldn't help but notice that you were a man covered in God's peace.'

I gulped. That was the very thing that Dave and Vivien had prayed for us the previous afternoon. 'Thank you, Lord,' I breathed silently.

He then went on to pray for Joshua and for me. I started to weep as his praying touched on the very same things about my future, virtually word for word, as had been prayed the previous evening by the group of Christians in the Schmittdiels' home.

'Lord this encouragement from You is too wonderful,' I prayed, as I really did feel peaceful again.

Daniel continued to share how God had answered prayer for the health of his own child, diagnosed in the womb with a condition that then reversed by the time of birth. The encounter appeared so angelic that I even wondered whether this man was for real!

The next morning at church, Dave Owen preached powerfully about being released from fear. The theme for many weeks had been about 'Choosing life', from the verse in Deuteronomy chapter 30,[35] and there were many aspects of this teaching that

---

[35] *Deuteronomy 30 v 15 – 20: "See I set before you today life and prosperity, death and destruction. For I command you today to love the Lord your God, to walk in his way, and and to keep his commands, decrees and laws; then you will live and increase, and and the Lord your God will bless you in the land you are entering to possess....This day I call Heaven and earth as witnesses against you that I have set before you life and death, blessings and curses. Now choose life, so that you and your children may live and that you may love the Lord your God, listen to his voice and hold fast to him. For the Lord is your life, and and he will give you as many years in the land he swore to give to your fathers Abraham, Isaac and Jacob."*

were helping me with the decisions we were facing. I did not realise how key this teaching was to become to me in later months, but God challenged my thinking a lot during that series.

In particular, I was challenged to see that death for the Christian is not defeat, but an embracing of eternal life. I started to pray and ask God that Joshua's own death would mirror this truth, that it would be a special triumphant event of him entering Heaven, rather than a dismal failure of disease getting the better of him.

The point Dave particularly drew out that Sunday was about listening to God's voice and holding fast to him. He expounded the theme by quoting examples of how doubt and fear come to challenge and intimidate us when we think that we have heard God on an issue. In other words, if there is one sure way of knowing you are on the right track, it is when something is thrown in straight away to try to rob you of your peace and pull you off course. Both Coral and I felt peaceful about our decision to return to the UK at the end of May, but complications with the next anaesthetic and flights to the UK apparently being fully booked all began to cast doubts on our decision. It was a wonderful test of our faith to hold on to the decision and not be panicked into something else. There was a sense of trusting God for Joshua's very life and it was exhilarating that we both felt God was saying the same thing.

This sermon hit me hard. I realised that my dilemmas over which date to return home were driven largely by fear rather than by the voice of God. In my heart of hearts I was confident that God had indicated the end of the month as the date for us to return to the UK, but listening to Joshua's noisy breathing at night was instilling fear in me and causing me to react with panic and lose sleep. After the service, I got someone to pray about this specifically. I felt a very real freedom come to my emotions and the clarity of hearing God's voice in the matter made the next few weeks an exciting walk of faith. The sense of panic finally dissipated from that point on.

Whilst still confident that God could heal him even now, I had not the slightest evidence that God had intended this for Joshua. Leaving Coral with the children that same Sunday evening, I drove Rebecca to church and on the way she expressed her feelings.

'If only God would tell us one way or the other what He is going to do for Joshua.'

I felt an inward pain for, if I was honest, I had discerned that God was not going to heal Joshua, but take him to Heaven. I was in the process of surrendering my will to God's will in the light of this likely eventuality. But it was too painful to express that there and then. Joshua was a gift from God. At times my love for him and my own self-protection caused me to cling on self-ishly, rather than release him to God. Now in the ultimate surrender, I was needing God's help to get to that same attitude at a deeper level.

Monday morning arrived and I bundled Joshua into the car as usual for his dose of radiation therapy. Most mornings he and I held the same conversation:

'Go hopals Tim? See Carol - see doctor Sachs?' Joshua would ask quizzically.

'Yes Joshua. Joshua is going to have a little smelly gas, Daddy will stay with you. You'll have a little sleep.'

'Oh,' he would reply. 'See Sarah, Daddy?'

'Yes Joshua, we'll see Sarah in the recovery room when you

wake up.'

'Oooh.   See Sempit Tim - Have bekfast?' he would coo in anticipation.

'That's right Joshua.   When you've woken up we'll have breakfast, you can watch Sesame Street on the television and Daddy will get you dressed.   Then we'll come home and find Mummy and Misha.'

I loved these little conversations with Joshua. It was great seeing his memory develop and his ability to make associations. It was a very rewarding part of his development. I had also got used to seeing the surprise of other patients and staff as they realised that it was Joshua and not me, who was walking into the Radiation department for treatment. Some of the other patients became very attached to Joshua and even bought him presents. He showed no fear and called the treatment room his 'bedroom'.

'Hi, I'm back.   Where Joshla's bedroom?' was a frequent greeting from our intrepid young man as he entered the department. His cheeriness seemed to brighten the otherwise sombre atmosphere of patients awaiting their treatment where children were rarely seen or heard.

'It's logical. It's where he goes to sleep - so it's his bedroom!' I explained to a puzzled Tony, the radiologist administering the treatment.   For his part, he could imagine more comfortable places to call a bedroom than the Radiation Room.

Joshua still didn't like his 'smelly gas' but his protest had become less and less each time, as he came to accept it. Maybe it was preferable to my singing! I would reassure him that I was there and of what we would do when he woke up and I'd generally keep talking until he was unconscious. So it had gone on week by week. Underneath I loathed having to put him through this. A blunt conversation was waiting for me this particular day with Kenny, the anaesthetist.

'Tim, I have worried about this all weekend. You are away from your family doctor, who would normally think more generally about what is the right thing to do. You have got to make a clear choice about what is best for Joshua. Ken is struggling to be blunt with you - none of us want this for Joshua - he is such a special little boy, but the truth is that radiation is not going to cure him. It has started working to a degree, but not as well as we hoped. At best it is only buying him time. You really ought to consider giving up and taking him home. Sometimes doing more for our loved one means doing less. Is this really being fair to Joshua? Anaesthesia twice a week and the tiredness from radiation is not giving him quality time; perhaps that's what you all need now. We'll continue for as long as you want, but promise me that you will think very hard about this.'

Sarah, the recovery room nurse, wept openly and hugged me as we left for Joshua's cubicle for Sesame Street and his breakfast.

Back home, Coral and I decided to make the following Friday the last dose of radiation, prior to our return to England the following week. Although we knew it was time to take this final step it unsettled her. She was pessimistic about Joshua's future but she dealt with the pain by shutting it out completely from her mind. While we were still in America she was determined to drain every last drop of enjoyment possible and focused on how best Joshua could do the same. Being part of this most difficult medical decision was almost more than she could bear. In contrast a strange sense of peace and excitement fell over me. I just knew it was the right decision.

'It's over to You now Lord - whatever the outcome,' I

resigned. There was only God left on the stage.

When that last Friday came, there was no denying the sadness felt by everyone. A retired couple who had befriended Joshua and me on our early morning visits for radiation left a big bag of presents for him. Carol, John and Ken were trying to remain their cheerful selves, but were choked. Ken prescribed some medicine for the flight home, saying that the high altitude might cause his airways to constrict further, but these injections through his Hickman Line half an hour before take off should relax the airways. I screamed on the inside! Another danger that I had not anticipated. He tried to reassure me by describing why suffocation was one of the kindest deaths for a child. I wanted to know such things but also did not want to know them, all at the same time. My drive to know as much as possible about Joshua's condition caused me immense pain at times. I couldn't blame Coral for wanting to delay facing things until she had to.

With our decision now made about when to leave Santa Monica, we were told that we would be unable to exchange our flight reservations for an earlier date. We tried to contact the pilot who had helped us on the way out, only to find that he was in Nairobi for the week! His girlfriend in London promised to get a message to him and to our amazement, he phoned a few days later to say that getting us tickets for the 30th or the 31st of May would be no problem, although he could not confirm until he got back to London on the 28th! We were delighted.

The extra days we stayed there enabled us to go once again to Disneyland and to the Knotts Berry Farm theme park, which Joshua thoroughly enjoyed, despite his waning energy. While we were there, Michael returned early from a ministry trip in India to be with us before we left and we were very moved and very pleased that he did this. We had kept in contact by phone and when he heard the latest piece of news he was very troubled and made arrangements to come home. So we were cramming in excursions for Joshua right until the last moment - Michael took us to an indoor soft play park and to the children's museum in LA as our final family treats.

At the soft play centre I made the mistake of leaving Joshua's hat at home and there appeared to be a school party there that day. There was no hiding the horrendous cancerous skin and distortion to Joshua's already birthmarked face, so the children's comments were inevitable. It had to be a miracle that here he was still the most self-confident little fellow, utterly oblivious to the stares. In truth, he still hardly heard any comments because he was too busy running off to the next activity. Once again, as Coral cradled Misha in her arms and watched what was happening to our son, I noticed that she was fighting back the tears. Unlike those that knew him, other children saw first the deformities and then later, if at all, the little person. There was no doubt Joshua had been shown everything he would have wanted to see in California. He had experienced more treats and more fun than others manage in all their childhood years and we felt very privileged to have had such opportunity.

It had been particularly precious to me to have this uninterrupted time with Joshua. As for most people, work was very demanding and costly of my time with the family. So I could appreciate these three months in California with him all the more. How glad I was that God had changed my reluctance to come to California by impressing on me that it was part of His plan for us as a family. We were very fortunate indeed despite the horrendous prospects.

Amazing things continued to happen for us up until the very end. Our neighbour had given us complimentary tickets to go to Universal Studios, but we ran out of time. Coral suggested that we give the tickets to Michael but I felt a caution about this. I prayed and sensed that I should give them to Grant Owen, Dave and Sylvia's son. When I handed them over, he was struck dumb. The previous evening he had felt discouraged and a friend had prayed with him and told him that he would be given some tickets within the next few days... A small 'coincidence' but it blew his mind and mine.

Things like that just happened for us during those months. I am convinced that there was nothing special about us - it was just God choosing to bless and encourage us abundantly - and the same God is available to everyone.

As our return date crept up on us we were increasingly aware that we did not want to go home. Usually after two weeks' vacation in the sun we would be ready for leaving but after three months in California we felt we were at home. The several days it took us to pack up our little home, return all the borrowed items and cancel telephone and television subscriptions etc. were very emotional and particularly so when visitors came to say their goodbyes.

Coral's grieving hit her at LAX airport as we waited to board our flight with Michael and Rebecca. She could hold back the tears no more. Joshua wanted to look in the shop and as he grabbed Michael's hand, she watched them walk off together and realised Joshua would never see his beloved Michael again. She turned to Rebecca who reassured her that she would visit us in England but we knew then that neither Rebecca nor Michael would see Joshua alive again and it was unbearable for Coral to watch Joshua's happy conversation with them both.

He seemed, as ever, blissfully unaware of what was happening to him. There were so many thank yous we had planned to say to these precious friends but neither of us could speak. Then it was time to go.

We walked through the metal detectors and regathered our belongings on the other side before walking on.   Joshua turned to wave goodbye again. We could still see Michael and Rebecca but Joshua could only walk a few steps before he stopped, turned and waved again, then he did it again and again. His unwillingness to just walk forward summed up our own feelings and it was as though he knew far more than we realised. We were far too choked to hurry him along or to give him any instructions at all.

Chapter Fourteen:
Facing the 'unfaceable'
Tim Recounts

We both knew we had brought Joshua home to die. Our time in California crystallised this for us as we saw the last hopes that medicine could offer fade away. We had also felt and seen the tremendous hand of God at work in our lives. As the going got tougher, so the measure of God's blessings on us increased all the more. His provision for us financially, materially, emotionally and spiritually had expanded our expectations and changed our outlook on life.

We had not lived in our own house for over seven months and coming back was completely disorientating. California had been the first quality family time we had had in a good while and the first and longest time Misha, now aged seven months, had been settled anywhere. Arriving home was like going through a time warp. Brand new Christmas and birthday presents were dotted around the house, which Joshua had great fun in rediscovering. All the clocks were still on winter time and needed putting forward in the middle of summer and even the electric blanket was still on the bed!

For Coral in particular, the knowledge that 'this was it' was devastating and anger came in like a flood. I too was struggling, although I had faced this eventuality over a longer period of time. When Dave Owen had preached in Malibu that everything to do with God pertains to life and life in its fullness, I knew we should also live from this basis, albeit looking into the face of death.

Even death then becomes a 'release into eternal life' for a Christian, rather than succumbing to the 'terminal event', as hospices prefer to call it.

We gained an appointment straight away at GOS to see Doctor Pritchard and his team and to update them on all that had happened in the States. That resulted in Joshua starting on codeine for continuous pain relief. Having reached the stage where we knew that to switch to palliative care was the right and best thing for Joshua, we declined all offers of further radiation, or experimental curative drugs. I think Jon was relieved that we had reached this point.

We had wanted to get Misha dedicated at church and had anticipated that it might be some weeks away before a convenient date could be found. To our surprise, our pastor could do it the following Sunday or the Sunday at the end of June. Neither of us felt confident about waiting a month; that was too far ahead, so with only a few days spare, we went for Sunday 9th June. We invited our families and friends to a barbecue and had a really special day. Joshua thoroughly enjoyed playing host and being reunited with his cousins. As the weather was gloriously hot, a good time was had by all. For one of the first times ever, there was no fear of Joshua being out in the sun and he was able to enjoy the water and fun.

That was the last full day of enjoyment and normality that he had. What perfect timing on God's part. No one could have known when Joshua would deteriorate and we realised then why our return date had been so important to get right. It was so perfect that everyone was able to see Joshua as his happy normal self. Had we waited any longer before returning, jetlag would have deterred us from holding the party so soon.

The following day, Joshua took to his bed and slept. We were devastated by the change in him. From then on he also refused all food. So began some very up and down days of sleeping followed by a morning or so of surprisingly normal energy and play. His confidence levels were shattered and he preferred to stay close. His decline in health and energy was all too sudden. We would long for him to wake up happy and active. One by one his usual play habits stopped and his energy declined until he preferred only to sit and watch his beloved Barney videos. We bought a video TV for his bedroom so that we could play Barney in the morning in an attempt to encourage him to wake up. He also thoroughly enjoyed watching the video footage we had recorded of our adventures in America. Occasionally, we found him switching on Barney at 4 a.m. and calling out, 'Drink a water with ice for Joshla!' Half asleep I would elicit a 'please' from him, comply with his request, only to be greeted with the question, 'Four ice Tim?' as he shook his cup to check.

'Don't be cheeky,' I'd reply. 'It's too early to watch television, you should be sleeping!' Despite the early hour I was delighted to have such interactions with him as this was the normal Joshua that we missed during his sleepy phases. Another time I went straight back to bed, only to be summoned ten minutes later. 'What do you want Joshua?'

'Put my cup by television, Tim.'

'Joshua, you could have done that if you sat up. That's naughty. Mummy and Daddy are trying to sleep!'

'Oh,' was the only sheepish response I got, but I had to laugh at his cheekiness.

He would often ask for a cuddle in the middle of the night, so I would climb into bed with him and he would chatter or poke my eye or nose. As he fell asleep again he would eventually roll over and bump into me and with a look of consternation and a prod say, 'Beep beep! Joshla's bed too small. Go back to Daddy's bed!'

Vivien Cunningham had dubbed him 'the little director' and how true it was! It was incredible that he was still managing to entertain us and make us laugh when we were all so exhausted and weary from the stress of watching our son deteriorate so. Most of the time he was so sleepy he seemed like a different character, just lying motionless on the beanbag downstairs or in bed upstairs; but every so often he still had a little surprise for us which made each day worth living.

Our local family doctor was excellent to us through this time and he started visiting regularly, as did our local paediatric community nurse, who had been a frequent visitor since we had brought Joshua home as a baby. The Symptom Care Nurse from GOS also joined us one day at home within the first few weeks and another gory shock followed. We had decided that we wanted to keep Joshua at home as long as possible, so we had to learn from the medics the likely scenarios we may have to face. As we listened to our nurse, we realised that we just had not been thinking along these lines.

'It's difficult to know how to broach the subject,' the nurse started.

'Tell it straight,' I replied. 'Be blunt.'

'The kindest thing would be if he develops pneumonia,' we were told and in comparison to some of the alternatives even suffocation would not be too traumatic. 'You must prepare yourselves for some nastier ends though. Some of them are more gruesome and no one can predict exactly how it will happen.'

The most frightening scenario described was of his tumours bursting a major blood vessel in the neck and either haemorrhaging externally or internally. Another thought that had not occurred to us was that he might suffer a stroke and possibly linger at length but without his full faculties.

What we were hearing was necessary for us to know, but the unexpected nature of the conversation made it all the more grisly. Then, my brain kicked back into gear with questions.

'But what if the tumours do rupture a major blood vessel in his neck. Should we call for an ambulance?' A prickly silence ensued.

'Depends,...I would say not,' was the reply. 'They will try to resuscitate him and you need to think what is kinder for Joshua. It would probably be better to call one of us, as we know him.'

I felt so sick. One would have thought that three and half years of hearing bad news had pushed us as far as we could go, but here was a new depth to plummet. Choosing whether or not to resuscitate your own son appeared an abhorrently hard decision. 'Oh God, help us! What should we do in that scenario?' Within a day or so, we had to face another similarly hard conversation.

As his windpipe kinked more under the pressure of the burgeoning tumours, his ability to clear the normal lung secretions was compromised and Joshua developed a mild chest infection. Our GP asked if we wanted antibiotics. Ordinarily that would have been an automatic thing, but he had joined the discussion about pneumonia being the kindest option and so gave us the choice. As Coral was so upset by the other gruesome options laid before us, she was questioning my instinct to give the antibiotic. 'What is the right decision here Lord?' I agonised. I was crying on the inside.

Suddenly Dave Owen's sermon of many weeks before flashed through my mind: 'All that pertains to God pertains to life. He is the author, the giver of life.' I also half remembered a Bible verse that reminds us that Jesus holds the keys to life and death:[36] it is He who decides when we die. These two truths gave me the answers I needed and relief replaced the anxiety. The weight of responsibility that my decision would determine the nature of my son's death lifted. God alone would determine when and how Joshua would die. His desire and will was for life and in that context I should do everything that would alleviate suffering and provide quality of life for Joshua. As his breathing was already noisy and difficult, a chest infection would only make matters worse and cause him greater anxiety, so it felt right to give the drugs to make him more comfortable. At the same time I realised my need to be calling on God's mercy that Joshua would not suffer unduly and that God would choose the most appropriate outcome.

June merged into July and the pattern of decline was chequered. Initially, Joshua weakened quite quickly. Then a surprising thing happened when we changed his pain relief to morphine. Instead of being even more sleepy, he started to have a good phase of wakefulness each day and this lasted some eight to ten days.

Then his breathing deteriorated once more. It seemed that if he got upset, he had a mini asthma-like attack, fighting for breath, which frightened him and the distress made it even harder for him to breathe. The first time this happened was during

---

[36] *Rev 1 v 18*

the night, so it was particularly distressing. Early the next morning I phoned GOS and the GP and they both arrived by
lunchtime. As he had shown such difficulty in breathing, they
advised us that he would be sure to stop swallowing soon too.
Just as I was recounting how ill he had been during the night,
Coral carried a bright and chirpy Joshua into the lounge. He had
woken up from his morning sleep exceptionally happy, had wanted to come downstairs, demanded and ate a big bowl of breakfast in front of everyone and generally did everything to make us
look complete liars!! Our Symptom Care nurse was brilliant
though and assured us that she believed us fully! Nevertheless,
none of us could believe our eyes. He was still surprising us, still
making us laugh and such a great transition in his apparent state
of health was unbelievable. Well - almost! During this time
phone calls from California, Memphis, Germany and all over
Britain reassured us that prayer for Joshua was fervently still
being pursued.

Joshua himself would ask us for prayer too.

'Do "nank you Jesus" Daddy,' he would ask (with Joshua we
called prayer 'saying Thank you Jesus') and remarkably, as we
prayed together, we would always see him visibly relax and his
breathing became more normal for a period. So Joshua was both
asking for and benefiting from prayer even though the obvious
and persistent prayer for his healing seemed to be ignored. Why
was this, friends would ask. Was God able to heal the cancer?
Absolutely. Was He choosing to? Obviously not. Did this freak
us?

It was devastating, heartbreaking and frustrating to see Joshua
suffer, yet somehow God enabled us still to trust Him. There are
so many mysteries in life and the question of a loving God allow-

ing suffering is one of them. Faith sometimes seems to mean accepting this, trusting God and not trying to solve the unsolvable. Of course we would have given anything for Joshua not to have gone through it. But somehow, God has enabled us to rest and trust in His absolute sovereignty. Do we understand why? Not entirely, but neither does that undermine our faith. Why try to reduce God down to the limits of our intellect?

The choking attacks remained a constant threat, so our life revolved around avoiding any upset. As water started to distress him, we had to stop bathing him. Nappy changes were causing him great distress, so we kept them to a minimum. Still he would get upset for no apparent reason. Then we realised that the morphine and cocktail of half a dozen other drugs were causing him tummy spasms. We learnt to quickly pick him up and reassure him as these began and in doing so, were able to lessen the severity of his breathing distress. Additionally, we learnt that we could give him Valium to help sleep at night and also to generally keep him a bit more calm. At times he would command, 'Call the doctor - get Pitchard!' and he was perplexed that we were no longer going to hospital. 'Hopals shut?' he enquired quizzically one day.

The waiting continued and although there were times of wishing it would all end, there were more times of hoping for just another interlude of energy and happiness. He had bounced back before and we kept praying for and waiting for another of those occasions. Meanwhile, we were predominantly housebound apart from the odd outing when Joshua could be persuaded. One of his last trips to church is a special memory. Our church had had three young Africans on its evangelism programme during the preceding year and for a brief period I had mentored one

of them. Liswe loved Joshua. For their farewell before returning to Zimbabwe most of the service was given over to them,
including some fantastic African worship singing led by Liswe.
Joshua loved it to bits. He kept walking into the aisle where he
could get a better view of the stage and half sat on my knee as I
squatted down. His whole body swayed and bopped with the
African rhythms and with his face aglow he would clap as each
song ended and say, 'Good song Daddy, good song!' Our emotions were so torn to shreds that this special moment was all the
more precious. Such simple, happy words from our son could
produce what I can only describe as very painful tears of joy.

In his last month of life he wanted cuddles more or less continually and was content to be held in our arms. In the last few
days, cuddles even became very necessary as the tumour mass
was so large and heavy in his neck, face and shoulder that Joshua
could not support his own weight. This, combined with the position of the tumour, meant that he could breathe more easily by
being upright with his head cocked back. His arms and legs had
withered to matchsticks and his torso had wasted away. Only the
hideous tumour grew, gorging on the nourishment his body
needed so desperately. Cancer is an ugly disease.

We took to holding him like this around the clock. Even
though I took the lion's share of the night shift, I did not mind. I
could see time was running out.

One final tough decision awaited me though. As words like
'pain' and 'sore' did not even feature in Joshua's vocabulary, we
agonised and argued about whether he was receiving sufficient
pain relief. Every time we spoke to GOS, the nurse would suggest increasing the morphine but I was unhappy with this. We
had visited a Children's Hospice and on reading one of the

nurse's drugs books I had learnt that too much morphine can be dangerous for those with respiratory compromise, as it deadens the impulse to draw breath. Early one morning I had indeed increased Joshua's dose of morphine significantly as directed and then had the frightening experience of noticing his breathing calm right down and occasionally stop unless I prodded him. It was an awful thing to feel responsible for and to watch this happen in the knowledge that my dosage had caused it. I checked with our GP and he confirmed that my interpretation of the incident was true, so I felt immense pressure. The stakes had gone to their ultimate height. The very drug we were administering to relieve his distress might even precipitate our son's death if we gave too much. We had the GOS nurse on one hand advising big increases and our GP urging caution on the other, with us in the middle. The 'right answer' depended on the degree to which Joshua was in uncontrolled pain. Whilst there was too much pain and too little morphine, an increase would be safe. When there was too much morphine and not enough pain to latch onto, we were in the danger zone. And WE were the best placed to judge his levels of pain. What was even worse; it was up to me.

Coral was unable to help at this time. She was suffering perhaps more now than at any other time. It came out quite often as anger towards me or towards God and in panic attacks. Any attempts to calm her down resulted in more anger. She needed God's peace more than ever but now she was too angry with Him and any one else close enough to receive it. She was in no state to help make decisions about morphine doses.

Yet I could not abdicate. Joshua was my son and my responsibility. There was nothing and no one to turn to other than to God. To have asked anyone to share the decision would have been unfair anyway.

'This is too hard Lord,' I collapsed. 'But I need You to help me get it right.' For the first time in Joshua's life I felt unable to rise to the challenge. I had nothing left to give. We had faced very tough decisions along the way, but this seemed the last straw. I was finished.

Chapter Fifteen:

Looking over the brink

Tim Recounts

During the night, in Joshua's bed, I held him and half propped him up, neither of us really sleeping. Even his voice failed and he could not breathe lying down. Speaking became more of a heavy breathing routine, but I could just about make out 'water' or 'nank you Jesus'.

At 3.30 a.m. Coral took over for a bit. I was exhausted. Coral enjoyed a very special time of just holding Joshua upright that night and she was glad that something caused her to wake up and come in. Unable to sleep herself in that position of holding him, she prayed a desperate prayer for Jesus to have mercy on our poor struggling son. This time was very testing and Coral's anger towards God was reaching fever pitch but it was reassuring to hold Joshua so close for a few hours and she found herself asking for God's help again. It was probably as much of a comfort to her as it was to Joshua himself.

When Misha woke at six Coral called our friend Joan Reynolds to look after her so that she could continue enjoying the longest cuddle she ever had with Joshua. Derek and Joan were leaders in our church and had known me since I started at the Grammar school where Derek taught Religious Education. I tried to sleep but couldn't. By this stage Joshua and Coral were downstairs and I was restless, wanting to be with them, so I showered, got dressed and joined them. Unusually too, Joshua seemed to want both of us with him (up until this point he had always been content with just one of us). That morning, if either of us left the room he would try to call us back but all he could manage was a faint 'Da' or 'Ma'. The weakening in his voice tore at our hearts. Over the months of decline we had constantly wished for and prayed for respite from his suffering and the 'just one more' circumstances. Each time we were lowering our expectations. 'Just one more time' running around, 'just one more time' of happy active play, 'just one more' conversation. And now even his speech was fading.

It was Thursday 1st August. As the morning progressed, my sister Ann and niece Becci arrived to relieve Joan. Together they quietly looked after the house and Misha while Coral and I took turns to hold Joshua. Our GP visited at about 11 a.m. and was visibly concerned.

'I don't think it will be long now, Tim,' he said and his eyes watered. 'It's taking him so much energy to breathe that his little body will tire out. He won't be able to sustain the effort indefinitely. Is his swallowing reflex still there?'

It was. Amazingly, Joshua was still taking his medicine down and managing to drink.

'He's getting weaker,' Coral and I said to each other almost simultaneously. We could both see it. All his ribs were showing as his muscles laboured to help him breathe. Even the veins were visible across his tummy. We continued to hold him upright while our own pain was now also excruciating. A conversation with a lady called Christine Noble nearly a year before about 'releasing Joshua into eternal life' was uppermost in my mind. She had quoted the Bible verse:

> *I tell you the truth, whatever you bind on earth will be bound in*
> *Heaven and whatever you loose on earth will be loosed in*

Heaven.[37]

She had reminded us that death is not defeat for a Christian. God's way of viewing death may not be the same as ours - more a releasing into eternal life. It was hard to take in at the time but now we had reached the point where Joshua's suffering was too much for him and us. I knew that I needed to pray and invite the Lord to come to be with us.

Just then our friend Rebecca in Santa Monica phoned (she was having a sleepless night) and Joshua just managed a quiet 'Hi' down the phone among his noisy breaths. She reminded us how he always asked for 'Joshla mucis [music] pease' whenever we got in the car. So, I dug out the 'Kids Praise' tape we had played so much in the States. Then I returned to the sofa where Coral was now holding Joshua. One of his eyes was closed from swelling down the left side of his face and the other was barely open so it seemed at first that he was asleep. He seemed to quieten and spoke no more. We just held him.

Coral started to cry. Joshua, throughout his life, displayed unusual concern and sensitivity to those upset, suffering or in pain. He would go out of his way to go and stand near, some-times touch the person, as if to say, 'I'm with you in this,' So remembering his sensitivity and suddenly noticing that he was not asleep after all but looking right at her, Coral apologised to him through her tears.

'I'm sorry Joshua. Mummy's crying for you because she knows you can't cry right now. Don't worry.' Then it was time for his Valium, but it remained in his mouth. His swallowing reflex had gone.

---

[37] *Matthew 18 v 18*

'Oh Holy Spirit come. Lord Jesus have mercy, come and be with us,' I prayed out loud over the three of us. It was a few minutes after two o'clock. Within thirty or forty seconds of that prayer Joshua stopped breathing.

'He's gone. His pupils have just dilated - they've just dilated. Did you see?' Coral sobbed. 'Oh Joshua, Joshua.' We both cried and cried. I called to my sister in the kitchen to phone for the doctor. Then Joshua's body sighed a couple of times which, for a split second threw us into temporary hope that he was still alive. But it wasn't to be.

The moment seemed surreal, except it was so very painfully real at the same time. The vividness of the moment will stay with us forever, but it was also an intensely precious moment of intimacy.

The tape recorder stopped. We hadn't really been listening - every faculty we possessed had been focused on Joshua's last fight for breath, but in the ensuing silence we realised the appropriateness of that last song: 'We're all children of the Lord' and particularly the line 'even though we're children, we're soldiers just the same.'

Joshua had been a fighter from his first to his last breath. Even his namesake in the Bible was a mighty warrior! How little we understood of the significance his name would hold when we chose it in Portugal, with Joshua barely more than a few millimetres big in Coral's womb and our having no idea anything was wrong. Did we chose it or did God just answer our prayer for choosing something appropriate for our 'yet to be born child'?

Very quickly Joan and Derek arrived to pray with us. We hadn't moved from the sofa, Coral still cradling Joshua's body, with me by their side. John and Dawn were already crossing the Atlantic to cut short their American holiday and John's ministry tour to be with us since they heard things were going very downhill for Joshua.

'Here we stand Lord,' Joan cried out in prayer, 'looking over the brink of eternity.' She repeated the phrase several times before moving on to talk and pray some more, as well as cry. She had a strong sense of the eternal perspective as she entered our lounge. The eternal is ever with us and around us. It's just hidden from our view by some invisible veil. On occasions we get but the slightest glimpse although the Lord wishes for us to be constantly tuned in to Him and His perspective.

Joan started to pray some more, but Coral stopped her.

'Joan, I don't feel like praying right now.' I was too dazed and numb to know what I wanted.

After a while the nurse and hospital consultant called round, then I took my turn at cradling Joshua, his body still warm. The next moment, Coral surprised me.

'Can we give him a bath and wash his hair? I've been itching to do that for weeks.' My initial reaction was to recoil, but sensitive to her needs, we went ahead. With hindsight, I'm so glad we did. We had done everything for him in life - as much as we could be trained in medically. He was our flesh and we had cared for him as we did ourselves. Caring for his body in death has filled my memories with a special intimacy of his passing. We ran a shallow, cool bath and together gave him one emotional last wash. Those hideous black tumours had spread down onto his chest and so invaded his tiny frame. We even put a clean dressing on his wiggly 'Hickman Line' before changing him into his favourite pyjamas. Then we laid him on his bed, where we and

relatives could grieve for him. My Mum soon arrived, as did
Coral's parents. We did not feel ready to let Joshua's body be
taken so we kept him on his bed until the next morning. Several
times we would go and talk to him as though he could hear us.
He looked so peaceful. I spent a lot of time that night holding his
little hand with the fat naevus finger, calling his name, weeping.
My son was gone and I was consumed by the vacuum he left
behind.

There had been nothing glorious about Joshua's suffering, but
his strong determination to live life to the full, even when it was
taking every sinew in his body to breathe, his stoicism in the face
of immense pain, his desire to the very end to ask where Misha
was, or where the last person to visit had gone - these things will
always cause us to thank God for the one very special, irreplace-
able person God chose to take to Heaven that day.

By morning Coral seemed to have come to terms with the fact
that the little body on Joshua's bed was no longer our boy. He
was there yet he was not there - he was with God and all we had
left was an empty shell, now so cold, hard and grey. It was like
a cruel tease to want to love and cuddle him but Joshua was not
there. It consoled her to think of him in Heaven, finally healed
of all his illness, happy and beautiful again.

For me though, I still held on to his hand - I needed to. Grief
hit me with a numbness. Tears flowed, but all emotion, even
pain, seemed to be sucked into a black hole with no name.
Shock, hurt, the sense of loss - my son was gone. I knew all the
Bible verses in my head about *'absent from the body is present with
the Lord'*[38] and so on. I had learnt to experience the truths of

---

[38] *2 Corinthians 5 v 8 (New King James Version)*

these scriptures when my Dad had died some five years beforehand. They had been a living comfort to me then - why not now?
And why didn't we sense anything of the Lord's presence at the
moment of Joshua's death? I was just numb. The only thing that
indicated to me that God had even been present was the timing
of the whole thing. It was as if my invitation to the Lord to come
and take Joshua was the thing that clinched it - the completion of
a circle. But I had felt nothing.

'Why?' I questioned God. 'I've been asking You to make
Joshua's death a special event. When You chose to take Elijah up
to Heaven, you allowed Elisha to see what was going on. Why,
after all Joshua and we have been through, didn't we sense Your
presence, even though we know You're always with us?' Silence.

But as I helped the undertaker place the corpse into the coffin
and carry it out of the house, that little body was still Joshua to
me and still felt my responsibility - I did not want to relinquish
him or it. As the undertaker's van drove away out of sight, with
my precious son's body in the back of it, I felt the wrench once
more and tears flowed. A hush seemed to come on the street, as
my brother-in-law Ian led me back into the house, weeping. My
own flesh and blood, gone. A massive hole had been hacked out
from my body in a jagged and unfinished way. The tear was deep
and the pain inexpressible.

The house started filling up again. First Coral's younger sister Donna came to help, then by lunchtime Michael had also
arrived from California. He just told his boss that morning that
he was going to England, got his friends to pray for him, then got
on the next plane. We were so glad that he would be with us for
Joshua's funeral.

That evening our friend Dave Simmons called by. Dave and

Amanda were due to go on holiday with their children the following day with another family we were close with, the Tizzards. Dave called by to say that he and Andrew Tizzard were prepared to cut short their holiday to serve at the funeral. Dave led worship at our church and Andrew Tizzard was our PA man so we were profoundly grateful to them for this offer. He asked us how we were feeling and suggested we pray. Coral couldn't hide her fury with God and his compassionate response became a main turning point for her.

'It's not my place to tell you what to do just now. I don't blame you at all for being angry, but God can cope with your anger Coral. He would rather you turn to Him with it, than turn away from Him,' Dave proffered in a choked voice. 'God understands your anger and pain. Don't let it become a barrier between you and Him, as He's the only one who can help you through it.' He was right, but at that moment Coral was still struggling.

I can hardly remember all the people who came to lend a hand with the normal things of life that week and our helpful visitors provided all the practical support we could wish for. Apart from the debilitating effects of the grief itself, the exhaustion of the preceding weeks was definitely catching up with us. Misha was still not sleeping through the night and, sensing something was amiss, she became clingy and more demanding than usual.

For quite some time I'd had a sense that Joshua was going to die. Over a year before I thought that God had spoken to me that he would take Joshua rather than heal him and that was part of what he was doing in Coral and me. I was gutted and questioned whether I had really heard God speak or was it just pessimism? Then in Malibu, on Mothering Sunday, the lead singer from the

60s band 'Hair' had sung 'Swing Low, Sweet Chariot' at Church and during the song I saw a picture in my mind of an intensely white and shining cloud mass gathering over the Pacific Ocean and heading for shore. I felt God impress on me that this was His glory gathering to come and take Joshua home. I was torn apart. Afterwards, the singer wrote to me saying how she had particularly chosen that song with Joshua in mind as she sensed that God was going to heal him here on earth, but somehow I wasn't comforted by her kind words.

Our friends back in Malibu had given us words of encouragement about our daughter and the stories of Elijah and Elisha seemed to crop up in this a couple of times. This had the effect of getting us to think of Misha as a special person in her own right, with a spirituality, ministry and future of her own. It also caused me to think a lot about the story of Elijah being taken up into Heaven in chariots of fire, Elisha watching this and receiving a double portion of the Spirit.[39] Since that point I had been praying for some special experience for Coral and me at the time of Joshua's death and now I was feeling cheated.

All of a sudden there was an uncomfortable gap in our lives. So much love had been poured into Joshua and the loving did not stop as suddenly as his death, so there was no object for all this emotion. The idea of transferring it on to Misha was impossible. We had loved her all along and she already had her own special place in our hearts. No, there was definitely a Joshua-shaped hole in our lives. We thank God we were able to cry and we continued to cry so much during those first days. On the one hand, we had known in our hearts that Joshua was dying, but we had

---

[39] *2 Kings 2 v 1 - 18*

lived for such a long time thinking Joshua would die 'at some
point in the future', we had almost come to believe it would
always be in the future. After all, he had survived for so long and
time and again come through crises that the doctors had not
expected. We had been lulled into a sense of enjoying each day
as though 'tomorrow' would never come. Even when our GP
predicted 'he would soon wear himself out with the effort of
breathing', there was no way that we could believe our little warrior would expire over such a 'normal' exertion.

In an instant our lives had changed and we were not the family we used to be. Would we ever get used to it? Our lives had
been so regimented around his care that for those first few days
in particular we caught ourselves going to mix his morphine or
draw up other medicine for him every few hours.

In the rawness of the moment even the memories of the good
times were painful, but it felt healthy to talk about him. It made
us feel closer together as we found ourselves talking in Joshua's
own funny little phrases as an intimate way of remembering.
Our love for him could somehow continue in this way, although
perhaps it was another way of holding on to a little part of him.
It was too soon to let go altogether. As memories were all we
had left of him, there was a desire to keep them alive to com-
pensate for the irrational fear that we would lose them also.

As Friday merged into Saturday, my 'black hole of grief' was
all-consuming, although his moment of death did hold a strange
sense of intimacy. I was still without any hope or assurance. All
the promises in the Bible about eternal life, about Heaven, about
God's love - they were all just words on a page. Again I prayed,
'Where were you Lord? Where are you? Why didn't you make
Joshua's death anything special like I'd asked You to? We felt

nothing of Your presence.' Silence.

I was very conscious of the choices facing me, either to turn to God and ask for His help, or to go it alone. I couldn't get the story from my mind in the Old Testament[40] where King David's young son dies. David's response was to go to the temple and to worship God. God had not healed David's son as David had pleaded, yet somehow David found it within himself to accept the outcome and get on with submitting himself to God. As I read and reread that story I realised that there was the precedent for me to follow, to strive to live up to. Even in the awfulness of grieving for a child, David was able to make God his main focus and worship Him. Although I felt anaesthetised through shock, I knew this was the way forward for me. It wasn't so much external behaviour as an inward attitude of heart, to consciously turn to God in prayer and worship and to look beyond the grief to embrace Him. As I chose to do this, I found God's comfort.

Looking back, I can recognise just how much God was with me at that point. Yet at the time, I didn't realise it and there was an utter emptiness and isolation, causing me to search desperately for a breakthrough. Coral was finding things much harder though and struggled even to turn to God through her pain and anger. 'God, help her...' became my frequent prayer. I could see her need, but had nothing to give. I could see no way to change this, unless God made something real for me. I was broken, blind and bankrupt, 'and I need You too, Lord.'

---

[40] *2 Samuel 12 v 15- 23*

Chapter Sixteen:
A birth into eternity
Tim Recounts

Although by the next day I started to thank God for Joshua's life and especially that his suffering was over, I could not help but feel cheated of the chance to be a Dad to him through his growing years. I had wanted so much to see him reach adulthood, to be a Dad and a best friend to him; to help him through the tough things that lay ahead with the medical and social challenges that his disease and appearance would present. All my dared-for hopes were shattered and I knew that I was still not grasping the positive reality of Heaven that the Bible promises for those who are Christians. I started to ask God to change this for me and felt that I should spend time in the Chapel of Rest reminding myself of the truth in scripture that he was now with God. Perhaps it would help me to release him into God's hands, where, in truth, he already was. I had to let go. I knew all the scriptures, but I still needed to hold his hand, cry, talk to him - his body was still 'Joshua' to me.

Coral found going to the Chapel too upsetting, The little distorted frame just reminded her of his suffering and she did not want to go back again after the first visit. So I asked John Singleton to come with me. John and I prayed for a while and I made a conscious effort to focus on the truths in the Bible about eternal life so I could use these verses in my praying.

As the hours went by, I realised that nothing had changed in the way I felt, that I had not fully accepted that Joshua was no

longer with us, or that he was with God. That evening as Michael
and I sat in the back garden talking, we decided to pray some
more. During this time the Lord gave Michael a very specific picture of Joshua now with Jesus, but he refused to describe it or to
talk with me about it no matter how hard I tried to persuade him.

'No,' he said, digging in his heels. 'I think it would be better
for you to get your own assurance from God and if this picture
of mine fits in with what God shows you, then so much the better. It will confirm to you what God is saying.' As I was no further forward, I determined to go back to the Chapel the next day
with Michael.

We got there just before lunch. Again I prayed. This time, as
I got up to leave, Michael encouraged me to stay and wait to see
what the Holy Spirit would do. We sat in silence.

I was open to this and waited. Then in the quietness, the
moments of Joshua's death replayed in my mind. But this time,
I got impressions of things as if looking through a darkened glass
wall, I was an onlooker to the events as they unfolded in our
lounge that afternoon. I saw myself put Joshua's favourite tape
on and kneel by Coral as she cradled Joshua on the sofa. His
whole body was contorting to draw each breath. As I saw myself
pray that prayer of release, asking the Lord and the Holy Spirit to
come, I saw in this 'playback' two bright shafts of light come
down to the sofa where we were sitting. Somehow, I knew these
to be the Holy Spirit and the Lord entering our room. As these
two very tall bright figures stood by the sofa, I saw a form, which
I knew instinctively to be Joshua, leave the little body in Coral's
arms to greet them. But to my surprise, a mighty warrior form
arose to greet the Lord. I remember feeling 'How can this be? Such
a mighty person inside such a tiny body?' The difference in stature

was incredible. It was like a cartoon of the genie and the lamp.

In this playback I saw the Lord speak to Joshua and say, 'Come Joshua, it's time. I've greater things for you to do now in My service in the Heavenlies. Come with us!' The three of them stood there, radiant and mighty in stature. The warrior Joshua looked back at the sofa at his mum and dad and replied, 'But what about Tim and Coral. Can't I stay with them a little longer?'

At this point in the playback I heard and saw the little body in Coral's arms sigh. The Lord replied to Joshua, 'No, your time here is complete - come with us. Come with us.' And the three of them left the room together and the little body in Coral's arms sighed one last time. Then the music stopped.

Still in the Chapel, this rerun of the moment of Joshua's death ended and I said to the Lord: 'But why didn't we feel Your presence with us at the moment of Joshua's death? Why was it so numbing and silent?' The reply came back to me, 'I don't know,' and we both laughed, for the inference was, 'Well, I was there whether you sensed Me or not - but your entire focus and faculties were naturally centred on your son and your grief. You were so consumed that you didn't notice My presence.'

Right there and then, I the sensed the Lord, the Holy Spirit and behind them the warrior Joshua enter the Chapel and I knew that Joshua was no longer in the body in the coffin. In this vision it was so graphically portrayed to me as he stood behind the Lord, that he was now 'in Christ,' complete, made whole and free from everything that trapped him in his little earthly body. Yet he was no longer able to communicate with me directly. The presence of the Lord in the room caused me to kneel down in silence before him. I felt the Lord continue and say to me, 'Behold your son, I am well pleased. Everything I gave you to do is complete, Tim. I only ever intended Joshua to be on earth for a short while, for I only needed a short time to build into your son all I needed for him to be complete in Heaven. Well done, your parenting of him is complete. There is nothing more to add. I will repay you, I will repay.'

At that point, myriad aspects of our rearing of Joshua, the lessons we had learnt, things people at home and around the world had prayed for him, all flashed through my mind and I knew that every single action and prayer had been a part of God building into little Joshua's character and spirit all that he needed to equip him for service in eternity. Things spoken and things unspoken. The transfer of the things of God in Coral and me into our child, added to by the prayers of so many. Small pieces of a giant jigsaw coming together rapidly to make a complete giant picture. Not one thing wasted, not one experience outside of God's will. Not one prayer or prophecy or encouragement outside of God's plan for his life. Even his suffering was allowed for a greater purpose and was part of his training on earth for service in God's Heavenly army. Every thread was woven in to make a complete tapestry. Utter divine fulfilment and perfection. Here was the wondrous transition from a life on earth to a fantastically glorious, exciting life in eternity. I could but glimpse the wonder of it all, as it tantalised my understanding. Here truly was Joshua's birth into eternity. Here was that special, glorious embrace of the eternal breaking into the sphere of time. In an instant my memory of Joshua's death metamorphosed into a celebration of inconceivable life in its fullness, far, far superior to our experience here on earth and yet very much coexisting with us here.

It was as if in this playback, the Lord had allowed the curtain to be drawn back on the natural would, for me to glimpse the activity and transactions going on in the supernatural - the eternal breaking into time. Eternity is not something waiting for us at the end of our life - it is all around us now.

After this vision I was left with the overwhelming sense that God now wanted the warrior Joshua in his Heavenly army and that his time on earth was fully complete. It was never meant to be any longer than it was. That knowledge had an immense healing and releasing effect on my grief and mourning. Since then I have not felt cheated of watching him grow up to maturity, as he has become in Heaven something of far greater value than human maturity can bring.

Before we left the Chapel, Michael began praying out loud and he said things like, 'Behold, my beloved son in whom I am well pleased'[41] as he felt that God was pleased with me and with my son. He continued in prayer by quoting the scripture that the Lord would 'restore the years that the locusts have eaten'[42], then while still praying he began to describe a vision of Joshua he had received the previous Sunday evening in our back garden, but had refused to share with anyone, of Joshua being a mighty warrior in the Lord's service with piercing eyes that perceived everything and yet who could still look at Coral and me and ask for, 'Cuddles Mummy! Cuddles Daddy!'

In an instant, my numbness was transformed into certain hope. The Lord had chosen to answer my prayer in a way that revolutionised me. I was humbled to have received such intimate and life-changing insight, all backed up by scripture and confirmed in the mouths of witnesses. Finally, Michael and I left the Chapel of Rest woozy from being in the presence of the living God.

---

[41] *Matthew 3 v 17* [42] *Joel 2 v 25- 27*

As we walked home across the park we bumped into Coral's close friend Ruth. 'We've just had an amazing time with God,' I called out. 'I'll tell you all about it later - we must get back to Coral.' Ruth said to us afterwards that our faces were glowing. She could tell that there was a dramatic change in the way I felt just from my appearance.

We hurried home, exceedingly late for lunch and I was anxious to write everything down so as not to lose any aspect of it. As time passed I worried about what others would think. Surely, it would be seen as the product of a highly charged, exhausted mind. I wouldn't be the first to have temporarily flipped in grief. But God had been gracious in confirming aspects of my experience directly to others.

As I told it to Derek and Joan, Joan reminded me that she prayed about 'the brink of eternity' moments after Joshua had died. As she had prayed over Coral and me, she had 'seen' three people walking away from our lounge into eternity. Michael's secret vision on the Sunday evening also matched my picture of Joshua in eternity on the Monday lunchtime. Then, as if to leave me in no doubt, our musician friend Andy Bradshaw wrote a song on the Sunday afternoon which he shared with John Singleton and me later in the week. I just knew it was God inspired as the words were so fitting with my experience in the Chapel;

Said a Father to his child
I'm going to call you to my side
I'm going to hold you in my arms
And wipe away the tears you've cried.
Your suffering is over
All you had to do is done

You gave everything you had to give
I'm so proud of you, my son
And the love you showed to all who knew you
Was so plain for all to see.
Said a Father to his child
Come rest in me.

Rest in me
Rest in me
Rest in me
Rest in me
Said a Father to his child, come rest in me.

Said a child to his Father
Watch over those I've left behind
Hold them in your arms
And wipe away the tears they've cried
Love them as you've loved me
Give them the peace given to me
Comfort them and show them it was all meant to be.
Said a Father to his children
Rest in me.
Said a Father to his child
From first to last you were mine
Your beauty, faith and innocence
Is preserved for all of time
And all the lives you touched will know
That greater things will come
You fulfilled every purpose
Precious beloved only son

And the grace that lived within you
Was so plain for all to see.
Said a Father to his child
Come rest in me.

Andy told me later that week that the words just flowed out of him as he sat down to write. He gave me the original scrap of paper on which he wrote them down and scarcely a word had been changed. He assured me that this was highly unusual for him when it came to writing lyrics.

When I was at a Promise Keepers conference in Los Angeles, the story was told of a South American pastor whom God was using significantly in his country. Many thousands of people were turning to Christ though his ministry to the extent that the drug barons were issuing death threats against him because their work-force and customer base was evaporating from under them as people turned to follow God for their direction in life. In the face of these threats, the pastor carried on his work undaunted. His response to those anxious friends and family around him was: 'I am immortal on this earth until I have completed all that God intends me to do here.'

That phrase struck me at the time as significant. Joshua was immortal on earth until he had completed all that God had given him to do. He was not taken from us prematurely, but his person-ality and character are now complete in Christ and greatly enhanced for His service, because he is free from his earthly body.

As I relayed the story of my vision to Coral over a now cold lunch, I could see she was excited about it all, but needing some reassurance for herself. 'Oh God, help her too…Make Yourself real to her as well,' I prayed silently.

Chapter Seventeen:
The Wedding Feast
Coral Recounts

A rrangements for the funeral were hectic. As this was the very last thing we could do for our son, we were anxious for it to be appropriate to him but also glorifying to God. Because Joshua had such a huge capacity for people I was keen that lots of his friends should take part. It was like organising our wedding service but cramming six months of planning into only six days. Somehow, with a couple of very late nights, it came together. God was in the plans, every one. We did not know it then but the finished result was the most powerful and uplifting service many people, including myself, have ever attended. We spent several evenings with John and Dawn Singleton, discussing, praying and trying to work out how God wanted the service to run. As it happened, some remarkable 'coincidences' came about.

Back in Malibu some three months before, Tim had felt that the story of King David and the death of his son should be used. Unbeknown to him and at about the same time in England, John had felt God impress him with the same scripture in connection with Joshua's funeral, whenever that might be.

We had both wanted Dave Cunningham to take part in the funeral, but could not see a way that it would be possible, as he wasn't in the country. An extra surprise came when, at the last moment, we heard that on their way home from Africa, Dave and Vivien Cunningham had managed to change their flight tickets to stay in England for a few days for the funeral. There was something very special and so obviously God ordained about them being with us. At times of crisis in California, Dave and Vivien were right by our side. It felt so right when Dave too agreed to take part in the thanksgiving.

Tim was really consumed with all these arrangements but I was often too exhausted to make decisions. I wanted it to be just right but at the same time, I was too engrossed in my own sorrow to think straight or to see how God was helping us. The strain was telling on me. Everyday easy tasks were seemingly too much and this meant even preparing meals became a pressure. I would be standing at the sink and a sudden rush of panic could overcome my body causing my heart to race and leading to shortness of breath. 'Oh no, I'm going to have a nervous breakdown,' I thought and as I worried about these symptoms they only got worse. I had to sit down and take some deep breaths. How utterly exhausted I was in every sense; spirit, body and emotions. I had absolutely no appetite and tried to avoid cooking. Then if Misha cried, often I had no emotional energy left to deal with pacifying her or putting her to sleep. Each time the phone rang was another pressure in case it was someone I did not really want to speak to and I never wanted to answer the door. These practical things were taken care of by having Michael in our house. He was just the right person who was able to take the initiative and 'muck in' when needed or be sensitive enough to know when to stand back. We even found that between the serious and sad moments we could have fun comparing Anglo-American nuances and making fun of each other's cultures. What was I doing being able to laugh within only three days of my son's death? I felt guilty. To laugh at all seemed out of place to me but it came naturally and had a releasing effect, as did the crying. My emotions were extreme on every level.

Before I knew it, the morning of the funeral had arrived and with all the arrangements made, I had some time for myself. When Misha was settled for her nap, I went into Joshua's room to be alone, to cry and to pray.

Tim found it hard to leave me alone; he knew I was at rock bottom and wanted to be with me, but at my insistence he eventually gave up and went downstairs to pray with Michael instead. At times like this I often want to shut everyone out, especially if I feel angry about a situation. Right then I was getting desperate. I knew it could become a barrier to intimacy between us if I kept pushing him away. But there are also times when I need space and this was one of them. We were about to bury my baby son and I had no assurance in my spirit that God even existed. I had been very encouraged to know that Tim had a real encounter with God during the week and I felt glad that he was feeling spiritually strong. The change in him had been obvious. If it had to be only one of us, I would always prefer him to be the strong one, maybe because if I feel weak, at least I can do something about it and I can be helped by him and by God. If he feels weak I feel totally inadequate. My weakness at that moment was a real weakness of faith. It just did not make sense that Joshua should have suffered. His going to Heaven I could cope with but suffering for such an innocent beautiful child? We don't know for sure how much pain he suffered or even if he really did, but the memories of him wriggling all night and day, seemingly unable to get comfortable and just trying to breathe were torturing me.

Why DOES God allow suffering anyway? It's a very hard question and the answers about suffering entering the world because of sin do not seem adequate to our human minds when the application becomes personal. I knew that I was not the first person in the world to dwell on this question and then begin to wonder if God is even there at all. In my lifetime I had spoken to many for whom this issue creates a total barrier between themselves and their loving Creator but although I never fully understood the reason for innocent suffering, I did not doubt that our God is a good God and totally just. I had always put it down to our own finite minds and not a question of God's goodness. But right then, I was at the end of myself and the doubts in my head were screaming louder than my faith.

'God, if you're there, just show yourself to me. I need to know you exist now more than ever before. Surely you understand that I need to KNOW Joshua is in Heaven like I always thought I believed. I need to really KNOW it.'

My favourite song by my friend Kate in California came to mind and I let the tears come as I remembered some of the words.

> *I need to know your touch*
> *I need to hear you call my name*
> *I need to feel your breath*
> *Upon my face, upon my pain*
> *If my hope grows old*
> *If my faith should ever dim*
> *If my love grows cold,*
> *Bring to me, the fire again...*[43]

I picked up my Bible and my 'Daily Notes' booklet of daily

---

[43] *Sung by Kate Miner. Words by Judie Lawson*

readings and expositions. I had not been able to read the Bible for over a week in my anger and confusion. Although I knew I was really struggling and needed God, all I could do was offer a quick prayer and rush off into activity. As is often the case I had given Him no time to answer me.

The last readings I had meditated on were about Job and his suffering and this was really still very appropriate. Yet strangely, I decided to skip all that and looked curiously instead at the notes for the day Joshua died. I wondered which part of the Bible the booklet would direct me to as I turned over to Thursday, 1st August. Then I almost shouted out loud. I wanted to call Tim but I stopped myself. For that day, the readings suddenly broke away from Job and turned instead to John 9! Of all the passages in the whole Bible, NONE had been more significant to Joshua's life than this story of the blind man who was healed 'that the glory of God might be displayed in his life'. We had considered this verse for the funeral service, but strangely it did not seem to fit now he was dead. Anyway, there were so many apparently more appropriate scriptures. So why, on the very morning of Joshua's funeral, was God directing me to John 9 again?!

Most importantly, it was proof enough for me that God existed! Something in my spirit leapt and danced. I was so excited to see that reading, of all days, printed for the day Joshua died by someone who had never even heard of our story. Surely God works in mysterious ways, but work He does!

There was more to come. As I thanked God for His encouragement, I thought I had no need to read the verses I already knew so well, so I read the Daily Notes booklet instead. Incredibly, the writer linked this story of the blind man to the dying and the terminally ill, even though there is no specific reference to death in the story. It may seem crazy but as I read these life-giving words and pondered on the 'coincidence' of it all, I was overwhelmed with inexplicable joy.

I carried on to read John 9 again anyway and this time in the New International Version, as I read *'but this happened so that the work of God might be displayed in his life'*. I asked God for the relevance and specific meaning to Joshua.

'Lord, show me something fresh from these well worn words,' I prayed and instantaneously He did. Suddenly I understood that the verse was still relevant. I realised that there was a reason I was reading it on such a significant day and that it meant Joshua's life would still display the work of God even after his death. All at once, precious memories of my special boy raced through my mind and I knew that although Joshua was gone, the memories of him still had things to show us about God. It was not over and that felt good. We had always felt that our son was something of a prophetic statement from God and here was confirmation. Why else would I find myself being directed to this verse all over again, even after Joshua had passed away? We would continue to remember different things about him and in the recollections the work of God would be displayed.

Through the hundreds of cards and letters received that week, so many people had commented on what a privilege it was to know Joshua. They would then continue with, 'He was so brave/lively/spirited/full of love/special/accepting of everyone/making the most of every minute/long suffering/never complaining/outgoing/confident and more.' In that quiet moment in Joshua's room, I realised that others would also have different personal memories of him and in each one could be a personal revelation of the Lord Himself. I decided to test this

thought and asked myself what was my own most obvious memory of him at that precise moment? Could it be something I
could attribute to being Christ-like? In my mind's eye, I saw
Joshua running to the front door every time the bell rang to welcome whoever was there. He never tired of excitement to see
someone coming into our house, even if it was only a workman
or electrician! He had room in his heart to accept wholeheart-
edly more and more people and they were more important to
him than any toy, food or television programme. He simply
delighted in everyone. What a picture of Jesus this was for me
and a real challenge too to be like that: so accepting, so hos-
pitable. In this way, I could see how Joshua could continue to
have an impact on my life and even on others, by remembering
aspects of his life and character and seeing Jesus each time we
did.

This was the 'glory of God' being revealed through Joshua's
life, which we had prayed for so many times in the last three and
a half years. It would not die and had not ended at the same time
as Joshua's life after all. This was just the beginning of a new time
and my excitement was really mounting as I realised I had hope
again. Friends and family were right to feel privileged to have
known Joshua, but how much greater was MY privilege that God
had chosen me to mother such an incredible child; little more
than a toddler, but he could teach us things about God's uncon-
ditional love both during his life and through memories. I felt
very humble. After all, only moments before I was beating my
fists on my Heavenly Father's breast in childish anger and frustration that He had not done exactly what I had wanted. In turn,
I received only loving encouragement back from Him. I was crying again but not from sadness or grief. Tim came back in and

this time I welcomed him to share my revelation. It was wonderful. I heard Michael downstairs open the front door and talk to our pastor John Singleton and Dave Cunningham about how upset I was right then, not realising what was going on in Joshua's bedroom. They came up to Tim and me with loving concern on their faces, offering to pray with us but were confused to see our faces shining and happy! This is the reality of the God we serve. When you really need it, He IS there and when He lifts you up there is no denying His existence. This was my very personal experience of God turning my tears to laughter. It was unmistakable. It was dramatic.

'You'll never guess what I just turned up in my 'Daily Notes' reading for the day Joshua died...' I showed John the reading for August 1st. He started laughing as he understood immediately the relevance of that verse and I loved seeing that he was as awestruck as I had been. I was ready to face the world with my head up. Joshua is in Heaven all right and the gift he was to us would continue to produce positive effect on our lives and others.

God's revelation to me was so timely and it gave me composure for the funeral. The Lord Himself had communicated to me that morning and I felt ready to tell the world! He had strengthened me as only He can, with encouragement and therefore a hope for the future. It was easy to walk up to the casket during the service and pray out loud before everyone. A day earlier, I could not have done it but right then I could thank Him from my heart without hesitation. God Himself had lifted me up and though I knew I would still grieve, still cry and still be sad, I knew I would not sink so low again. I would not doubt God's love and mercy to me whatever the circumstances. I could face my future grief with God, rather than being angry with Him.

It did not fully answer the question of suffering but neither did it need to anymore. I was totally convinced that God himself had 'spoken' to me. He loves me and has purpose for me, as well as having purpose for my son, however short his life was. To our limited human minds, some things of God are unfathomable but what was more important than working everything out was the ability to trust and have faith in my Maker again. He had given me that ability as only He can and I was no longer angry.

It was hot and humid outside as we followed the hearse to the church. High on top sat a three-foot-high statue of Barney in purple flowers which delighted local children who recognised him.

When we reached the church, the small white casket was carried on our friends' shoulders while another of Kate Miner's song's played clearly to remind us all where Joshua really was:

There is a place prepared for me
A table by the crystal sea
Where my beloved bids me rest
And gently lean upon his breast
He dries my tears, He breaks my chains
He binds my wounds, He heals my pain
He soothes my tired and troubled soul
He fills my cup - it overflow.s
The finest wine, the choicest bread
By his own nail scarred hands, I am fed
He hides my shame in holy dress
He clothes me with his righteousness
He lifts my veil, he draws me close
Proclaims me his to Heavenly hosts
While angels sing his reverence

He leads me in a sacred dance.
There is a place, by the crystal sea
Where my beloved, waits for me
He bids me come just as I am
To the Wedding Feast of the Lamb
To the Wedding Feast of the Lamb.[44]

John Singleton welcomed some four hundred friends and family, neighbours, medics and work colleagues to the church, some cutting short summer holidays and work trips abroad to be there and many making arrangements to stay overnight, leaving children at home. Joshua's little cousins and friends carried baskets of flowers down the aisle to lay at the casket. The youngest was barely four years old himself.

So many people, yet all familiar, supportive faces although several were clearly anxious that they might fall apart with the proceedings about to start.

'It must be hard to be here if you don't know Joshua is in Heaven as I do,' I thought. And here am I at peace and so honoured that such a number of people have come. I smiled and felt peaceful.

John encouraged everyone to put aside the inevitable questions we would have over Joshua's death in favour of receiving the word of God. 'We could choose to believe to receive.' Yes, I thought to myself, you're spot on!

'The special ministry of God's grace goes way beyond our natural understanding,' he continued to the packed church and I almost wanted to shout 'Amen!'. The occasion and of course my

---

[44] *Sung by Kate Miner. Words by Judie Lawson*

English reserve stopped me. Every hymn, every song, was charged with such truth and meaning even from the start as we sang first 'How great Thou art'. I know Tim chose this hymn for its powerful focus on the sovereignty and greatness of God but one verse especially significant to me was;

And when I think that God, His own son not sparing
Sent him to die, I scarce can take it in

The reading from 2 Corinthians 1 verses 3-11 also summed up how we felt, particularly the verse,

Indeed, in our hearts we felt the sentence of death. But this happened that we might not rely on ourselves but on God, who raises the dead. He has delivered us form such a deadly peril and He will continue to deliver us. On Him we have set our hope that He will continue deliver us, as you help us by your prayers.

My friend Ruth Botterill led the time of thanksgiving by first reminding us about Joshua's very unique little character.

'We mustn't let the deep pain of losing Joshua overwhelm the special memories we have of him,' she advised us, producing a couple of his favourite toys and I was riveted.

'Joshua loved phones and especially mobile ones as he was always on the move. Not only did he learn the power of dialling three nines but his favourite trick was to 'talk to lady' as he called it. You know, the voice which says "The number you have dialled has not been recognised. Please hang up and try again". Joshua always did - again and again! Joshua also had a special talent for bringing down barriers between people. You could not stay aloof for long with him around as he made you wear his policeman's hat or chase him on all fours like a dog, or even just sit on the floor with him, so he could jump straight up and run away!'

The picture she put across was of someone young and fun loving. Yes, that too could be a picture of our Lord, I thought. Why do we think of God with white hair and a walking stick when His obvious creativity and 'never sleeping' points to a much more energetic, vibrant person. Dave Cunningham then rightly pointed out that this was not a sad time for Joshua. It was his coronation.

'Life is not according to number of days, it's according to purpose and Joshua's life was full of purpose. He is probably 'directing' now in Heaven.' Again I wanted to shout 'Amen!' as I felt such strong agreement with all he said. These were no empty words, nor purely emotional encouragement (although Dave himself struggled to speak for his own tears). He was bringing biblical truth, the word of God and continued: 'A number of times I looked into those piercing blue eyes of Joshua's and I could almost hear his spirit screaming; "This tent cannot restrain me because I am alive in Jesus".'

There was no denying the presence of God in the church that afternoon. Much of what was said and sung was a serious, significant, poignant expression of the heart to God, but there was no heaviness in this service. Even the very atmosphere was right and suited to our special little man. As Paul Oakley's song 'Jesus Lover of my soul' expresses it:

It's all about You Jesus and all this is for You,
For Your glory and fame.
It's not about me, as if You should do things my way.
You alone are God and I surrender to Your ways.[45]

[45] *Jesus Lover of my Soul, It's All About You, Paul Oakley., Copyright © 1995 Kingsway's Thankyou Music, P O Box 75, Eastbourne, East Sussex, BN23 6NW, UK. Used by permission.*

John preached a short message on King David's response to his baby son's death and reminded us that as every word in the Bible is there for our comfort, encouragement and instruction, we could use the story today to show us what our own response should be to Joshua's death.

While the child was still alive, I fasted and wept. I thought, 'Who knows? The Lord may be gracious to me and let the child live. But now that he is dead, why should I fast? Can I bring him back again? I will go to him, but he will not return to me.[46]

'Death is not without pain but neither is it finality or the destruction of our hope,' said John in his address. 'It was clear Joshua himself knew Jesus, despite his language not being fully developed. His requests to, 'Do nank you Jesus,' which became even more frequent towards the end showed us something in his spirit was reaching out to his God. As Tim and Coral have a relationship with God through Jesus, they are assured of their own place in Heaven one day and that they will reunite with their son.'

As we left the church for Joshua's committal at the cemetery, we felt curiously full of joy and hope. Even as the last song was played over the PA system it was as though Joshua himself was there, urging everyone to come and know the Lord as he did;

We're all children of the Lord...
And even tho' we're children
We're soldiers just the same
Come to the Lord as children

---

[46] *2 Samuel 12 v 22 -23*

And praise His name[47]

Over two hundred people joined us for refreshments after the burial. Our guests spontaneously queued in one long line to greet Tim and me personally. It felt very special to have everyone close with us and to be able to exchange at least a few words with them all.

'This feels more like a wedding reception than a funeral,' Tim and I said almost simultaneously to one another as we paused for breath.

'It is,' interjected Tim's sister Ann on overhearing us. 'It's the wedding feast of the Lamb. Joshua has taken his seat and he and all the others in Heaven are just waiting for the rest of us to join them there.'

---

[47] *Children of the Lord, Bob Bennett. Copyright © 1978 Maranatha! Music. Administered by Copycare P O Box 77 Hailsham BN27 3EF. music@copycare.com*
Used by permission.

Chapter Eighteen:
Healing through grieving
Tim Recounts

The high of Joshua's funeral and the dramatic spiritual encounters we both experienced individually in the Chapel of Rest and in Coral's Bible readings could make a suitable ending, but it would be incomplete not to reflect the reality that followed. Some platitudes imply that we shouldn't grieve as Christians, as we believe that we will go to Heaven when we die anyway. Being a Christian - that is, knowing God personally through surrendering the rule and authority of our own lives to Him - is not an arrogant statement that we exist on some kind of superior plane to anyone else. For us, it just means He helps us. We would never support the theory that Christians have no need to grieve. Having released Joshua into eternity, we needed to readjust to the present.

Like any significant bereavement, the full impact of our loss would take months to surface completely and we knew it. The process of turning our pain over to God has been iterative, not a 'one-off' event. The tremendous help that God gave us in those early days would continue to sustain us through the tough times still to come. So we are not ashamed to admit to a time of mourning and we do not pretend that it was over in a week. In Psalm 51 King David speaks about God *'requiring truth in my innermost being'*,[48] and that was our starting point.

Throughout the Psalms David demonstrates a very open relationship with God about his reactions to circumstances and people. Coral and I both found this openness before God to be a successful prerequisite to receiving God's healing for our own pain. Suppressing emotional hurt does not resolve it and I was relieved that Coral did not follow her natural tendency to do that now. Having watched a friend become suicidal as unresolved grief resurfaced a year later, she recognised the importance of allowing herself to grieve. She even went so far as to actively work against her natural instincts to bury the pain. It was not a time for pretending to be happy.

'I'm taking my medicine,' Coral told our close friends when they asked how she was doing. 'It's not pleasant to reminisce and be sad so often but it's a necessary thing for me to do. I can't say I'm fine if that means happy, but it feels very healthy to face it now. The sooner I work it through, the sooner I can get out the other side. Just ignore me if I cry a lot. It's all part of my healing.'

She saw it as a job to complete, which, for my task-oriented wife, was really a very positive way of approaching this time. Doctor William A Miller summarised it beautifully for her when he wrote *'Grief is good medicine for the sickness of loss'*[49] Our goal was to progress back to emotional wholeness. Like any rational person, we did not wish to dwell in this 'season of mourning'[50] any longer than was necessary. The Bible does not condemn

---

[48] *Psalm 51 v 6* [49] *When Going to Pieces Holds You Together - 1976 Augsburg Fortress Publishers, Minneapolis Minnesota. Used with permission.* [50] *Ecclesiastes 3 v 1-4: "There is a time for everything and a season for every activity under Heaven. A time to weep and a time to laugh, a time to mourn and a time to dance." Ecclesiastes 3 v 1 - 4*

grief, therefore God would surely help us through it.

Although we struggled to find much good Christian material on this subject, the classic *A Grief Observed* by C S Lewis.[51] was just the powerful personal testimony we were in need of. It provided us with much reassurance that our approach to bereavement was also a godly one whilst it avoided self-pity.

One most poignant conversation ensued with Pete Parris, when he shared with us how he mourned the loss of his wife Brenda.

'Allow yourselves time to grieve,' he encouraged us. 'Don't try to shut it out. You will find that God will lead you and it will not last forever. When the time was right, I felt God drew my grief to a close and now I can honestly say it is finished.' A glimpse of excitement and faith was born in us that day and a sure hope that God would not allow our own intense pain to last a lifetime. It was OK to feel as awful as we were feeling. The voice of experience was telling us that it would end and this was a powerful testimony to God's faithfulness.

Along with our reading, the next weapon in our armoury was our family and friends. On the evening of His arrest, trial and crucifixion, Jesus Himself took his disciples into the Garden of Gethsemane with Him. He asked the three disciples closest to Him to go further still, as He faced His hardest test.

My soul is overwhelmed with sorrow to the point of death. Stay here and keep watch with me.[52]

The desire to be with those you are close to has a worthy precedent. In bereavement, withdrawal is a common reaction.

---

[51] *1961. Published by Faber and Faber Ltd, 3 Queen Square, London, WC1N 3AU, UK.*
[52] *Matthew 26 v 38*

We were not easy company, as our pain and anger made us 'prickly' and volatile. Yet we longed for close companionship and we first needed to relearn how to provide that to each other. Death is about separation - temporary though that is for the Christian. The withdrawal by friends compounds the separation experience. It is a lonely, even isolating time as those around struggle to comprehend how you are feeling and everyone around you is terrified of saying 'the wrong thing'. It is a very intimate pain, which those outside our very closest friends could not touch; yet most people wanted to acknowledge it in some form. Even so, among those who tried, what we found most helpful was 'How are you doing?' The 'I know how you feel' statements were well intentioned but made us angry. We soon realised we were becoming separate from most people around us and consolidated to just one or two 'good listeners'. Even then, there were some things we simply had to walk through alone. In Gethsemane only Jesus could go through what He was facing. There was no sharing it or delegation. It was 'His cup' and no one else could experience that pain:

My Father, if it is not possible for this cup to be taken away unless I drink it, may Your will be done.[53]

Of course, this was also a reminder to us that Jesus chose not to walk away at that point and we too needed to remain surrendered to God in our grieving. Our responses would always be our choices and our responsibility. The whole issue of God's sovereignty remained key. Whilst we remained accepting of God's decision to take Joshua, we experienced His comfort and

---

[53]*Matthew 26 v 42*

strength. When we fought against it we ended up in fruitless self-pity and frustration, for we couldn't change the outcome.

There was still another hurdle I needed to cross. Since the powerful vision God gave me in the Chapel of Rest, a sense of completeness about Joshua's life persisted. I genuinely believed I had released him but it still hurt. It did not make sense that I could feel excited about Joshua's place in eternity and experience the peace of God at the same time as such emotional pain. I had accepted what had happened to Joshua but now I needed to accept what had happened to me.

It took a few weeks for the worst deluge of pain and reaction to hit me. By mid August my emotional anaesthetic had dissipated. I wanted my son back, just for one last hold. My arms ached for him relentlessly, almost physically. Coral and I drew back from one another, unable to go beyond surface reactions to touch the pain in each other. Both of us were bankrupt, like two vacuums colliding together, wanting to be filled but only hurting each other more. How easily I understand why couples so often do not survive the strain of losing a child. The stress of bereavement seems to exacerbate every fault line in the relationship. Every personality trait you dislike in your partner appears to be in your face constantly. We both felt so brittle that communication deteriorated to treading on eggshells or all out war. We had to reconcile but were choosing not to for a while. As the numbness, shock and denial wore off, the hurting left behind was intense. Together with fatigue, our different reactions to the same pain had an explosive, negative effect on our marriage. I was feeling raw and over-sensitive while Coral appeared to show flippancy and a shrugging off. When her nonchalance trampled across my pain, a few chosen but cutting words from me in return would trigger an unhelpful scene. As our differences became huge, the most awful row erupted between us. Even a session with John and Dawn changed things little until we reached the point of deciding to commit to work through together as partners, rather than as enemies. It was a very practical decision for me to say goodbye to my self-protection against Coral's aggravating response.

Some of the teaching from the Promise Keepers conference in LA about removing the barriers to communication in marriage was unwelcome but an accurate reminder of what lead I should be taking. I had to learn to forgive Coral and turn to God for the salve to my pain that she was unable to provide. The spiral was broken. In turn, Coral uncharacteristically reached out one day for a hug as a wave of tears broke across her out of the blue. As I reciprocated I felt a new tenderness in response to her vulnerability. I began to see past her superficial reactions and recognise the level of pain she was feeling underneath. We started to rebuild our relationship, making most progress when we made a commitment to each other at the expense of our own needs. It was surely God's way - selfless rather than selfish.

Looking after baby Misha was a tonic to our healing but it did not cure the ulcer of our loss. We were so grateful to have our beautiful daughter but Coral particularly missed the special position that went with being Joshua's parent. Lots of mums have healthy children. Suddenly there was a new family life with no hospital visits, routines of creams and bandages. At the birth of our son the prospect of a semi-hospitalised life seemed like a prison sentence but when it was gone, we missed it and that felt ridiculous. The 'normal family life' that everyone told us we didn't have with Joshua was utter abnormality for us now he was gone.

We both felt redundant. For Coral, there was a deeper longing associated with this, as caring for Joshua had provided her with a sense of purpose as well as identity. The redundancy she had taken from her job a year before caught up with her. Without Joshua she felt redundant on every level and this expressed itself in feelings of uselessness and lethargy. She had felt so important to Joshua's wellbeing that anything else in her life came second. This had placed an abnormal balance on our relationship, which now would take months to readjust.

I too suffered a loss as dad to Joshua, carer and fighter on his behalf in the medical world. Not having a specific role in the office at first reinforced that sense of loss when I returned to work. I felt suicidal. Although no one knew it, many a day started with me staring at the electrified rails and wishing I were under the train rather than on it. I just did not want to live any more. Thoughts of Coral and Misha kept me focused on living. However, I needed structure to my day and a sense of fulfilment but on reflection, we both recognised that the stuffing had been taken out of us and we needed time to adjust. For me, that meant a quieter existence at work than I was used to.

'If you have any spare energies right now Tim, you need to be giving them to your wife and child, not the Bank. There'll be plenty of time for that in the future. You can't go through what you have without realising what is important in life.' My boss was right.

So, after a career of high challenge I found a role that allowed me to work on my own from home or the office. I had a moderate sense of achievement but more significantly, I could choose where to be and spend more time with Coral and Misha. We cherished this quiet existence, re-establishing our lives in our shrunken family. We withdrew socially and concentrated on honesty between each other and with God. We needed time to allow Him to 'restore the soul'.[54]

As time moved on we both suffered a sensation which the text books describe as 'yearning' or 'searching'. We felt restless and frustrated and wanted change. We thought about moving house, but knew that wasn't the answer for us. As part of our drive to confront grief, we decided to go back to places that held special memories of Joshua, to 'face' the memories we had of him. Whilst this was often painful, it became very therapeutic. Naturally, one of those places had to be California.

Stepping off the plane, we realised that this was not so much a holiday as a 'pilgrimage', or a return to somewhere we used to live. Our emotions were in turmoil. Where was Joshua? It did not feel right that he was not there with us and we kept expecting to hear his little voice in the back of the car. At times, the two weeks we spent there were excruciating. It felt as though all the 'good work' we had done on our grieving at home was now being undone. However, as the time passed, we became aware that it was a healing time. Grief is not a steady upward curve like we had expected. It is more like a bumpy road where occasional unanticipated crevices cause you to doubt the progress you have made. To avoid these unpleasant experiences would only be to delay them.

When we returned to California for the second time, the experience was entirely different. Happy memories abounded but without the baggage of pain they carried before. We suddenly realised God really was healing us. We were regaining strength and wholeness. Any fears we entertained of our grief

---

[54] *Psalm 23*

never ending were dispersed as we delighted in the progress we had made.

About six months after Joshua's death, I took a more appropriately challenging role at work, in recognition of the restoration I was feeling inside. By this stage most of the emotional pain had subsided and resilience was restored. It took a few months more for enjoyment of life to be restored.

Coral would describe it as emerging from grief - realising that there is a life beyond perpetual sadness where intense pain no longer consumes all joy of life. We both found that our memories sometimes were unexpectedly a little sore, but more usually, we remembered Joshua wistfully. The hard moments, or occasionally days, always pass and each time we approach a significant anniversary date, we brace ourselves for the 'medicine'. Through all the pain, hardships, frustrations and tears, if we could select the specific path of our lives; neither of us would ever choose to leave out the part that was Joshua or the precious lessons God taught us through him.

One of my main conclusions from this experience is God's desire for us to have a mature understanding of His sovereignty. To be people who are not shaken by personal or societal circumstance, but who find rest in His Lordship. Hard things continue to occur in individual's lives and the world continues to face uncertain times. God needs spiritual adults, not just spiritual adolescents, to do His bidding in the earth. People who make godly decisions in their personal and corporate lives. He is calling His church to rise up as His mighty warriors, united and mature, submitted to His leading. There is a world, there are people, who need the good news of the gospel, who need healing of their bodies, minds and spirits. We need to be focused and stripped of unnecessary baggage in order to respond fully to God's command.

> *The Spirit of the Sovereign Lord is upon me because the Lord has anointed me to preach the good news to the poor. He has sent me to bind up the broken-hearted, to proclaim freedom for the captives and release for the prisoners, to proclaim the year of the Lord's favour and the day of vengeance of our God, to comfort all who mourn and provide for those who grieve in Zion - to bestow on them a crown of beauty instead of ashes, the oil of gladness instead of mourning and a garment of praise instead of a spirit of despair. They will be called oaks of righteousness, a planting of the Lord for the display of His splendour.* [55]

In His final commission, Jesus requested that we take this good news of His to those who need it. So many aspects of what we went through reminded me of the reality of the gospel. Our experiences with our son were but faint shadows of some aspects of what God the Father and Jesus went through at that first Easter in order to make it possible for us, mere humans, to know God personally. We experience sustenance from that divine relationship in our own lives but more than that, we are assured about eternity. There is a life after this one, one for which we make the choices now. As a result of what Jesus did and for those who choose it, that will be as it is for Joshua, something far superior and greater than we can ever imagine. And the transition? For those who love Jesus, it is not their death: it is their birth into eternity.

---

[55] *Isaiah 61 v 1 - 3*